ENCOUNTERS WITH NATIONALISM

ENCOUNTERS WITH NATIONALISM

Ernest Gellner

BLACKWELL
Publishers

First published 1994
Reprinted 1995, 1996

Blackwell Publishers Ltd
108 Cowley Road
Oxford OX4 1JF
UK

Blackwell Publishers Inc.
238 Main Street
Cambridge, Massachusetts 02142
USA

British Library Cataloguing in Publication Data

A CIP catalogue record for this book is available from the British Library.

Library of Congress Cataloging-in-Publication Data
Gellner, Ernest.
    Encounters with nationalism / Ernest Gellner.
        p.   cm.
    Includes bibliographical references (p.) and index.
    ISBN 0–631–19479–7 (acid-free paper). — ISBN 0–631–19481–9 (pbk. acid-free paper)
    1. Nationalism.   I. Title.
JC311.G47   1994
320.5′4—dc20   94–1737
                                                               CIP

Typeset in 11 on 13 pt Plantin
by Graphicraft Typesetters Ltd, Hong Kong
Printed in Great Britain by T.J. Press Ltd, Padstow, Cornwall

This book is printed on acid-free paper

Contents

Preface

Sir Henry Maine's famous formula – *from status to contract* – has been taken by many to offer the most succinct summary of the nature of the transition to modern society. But it seems to me that he might just as well have said from status to *culture*. Agrarian society is indeed largely a stable system of ascribed statuses: but culture, with its richly differentiated and almost endless nuances, is used to underwrite, render visible and reinforce those statuses. Its subtle differences mark off social positions. It helps make them legitimate by causing them to be deeply internalized, and it eliminates friction by making them highly conspicuous. But shared culture does *not* create wide-ranging bonds, and does *not* underwrite political boundaries.

Modern man enjoys, or suffers from, no such rigid and reinforced ascribed status. He *makes* his own position, not by a single contract, but by a vast multiplicity of minor contracts with his fellows. In order to negotiate and articulate these contracts, he must speak in the same idiom as his numerous partners. A large, anonymous and mobile mass of individuals, negotiating countless contracts with each other, is obliged to share a culture. They must learn to follow the same rules in articulating their terms. Cultural nuance no longer symbolizes status, for the status is no longer given: but a shared, standardized culture indicates the eligibility and ability of participants to take part in this open market of negotiable, specific statuses, to be effective members of the same collectivity.

So a shared *high* culture (i.e. one whose members have been trained by an educational system to formulate and understand context-free messages in a shared idiom) becomes enormously important. It is no longer the privilege of a limited clerical or legal stratum; instead, it is a precondition of *any* social participation at all, of moral citizenship.

It is this new importance of a shared culture which makes men into nationalists: the congruence between their own culture and that of the political, economic and educational bureaucracies which surround them, becomes the most important single fact of their lives. They must be concerned with that congruence, with its achievement or its protection: and this turns them into nationalists. Their first political concern must be that they are members of a political unit which identifies with *their* idiom, ensures its perpetuation, employment, defence. That is what nationalism is.

Yet nationalism is not the only character on the ideological scene. Men are or are not nationalists, but they also have their attitudes to religion, to traditional institutions, to the imperative of economic development, to the issue of the availability of universal truth or, on the contrary, the validity of relative local truths. Positions adopted on these issues can be combined with nationalism, or be in conflict with it, in a wide variety of ways. They have their elective affinities and repugnancies, but there is more than one pattern of alignment.

These essays examine the involvement of diverse thinkers who have well-developed positions on the issues, with nationalism. Several consider the confrontation between nationalism and Marxism; one of them (chapter 1) follows up Roman Szporluk's thesis that Marxism was, from the very beginning, engaged in a rivalry with nationalism concerning which of the two was the more effective method of economic *rattrapage*, and that Karl Marx was, in the *Communist Manifesto*, covertly polemicizing with Friedrich List, the prophet of development in the service of nationalism, and of nationalism in the service of development, and of the claim that, in the end, Marxists became crypto-Listians. The essay on the transition from kinship to ethnicity (chapter 3) was written in the erstwhile Soviet Union, at a time when local scholars still had to go through the motions of being Marxists; it attempts to highlight the fact that the under-estimation of nationalism was a mistake shared by liberalism and Marxism. The work of Miroslav Hroch (chapter 14) represents a remarkable attempt to superimpose the Marxist and nationalist visions of history on each other: history is the account of changing class relations *and* yet the independent reality of nations is also conceded and affirmed. Moreover, he brings to his aid a wealth of historical and sociological documentation, and the case must be taken seriously by someone who, like myself, accepts *neither* of these two visions.

The essay on E. H. Carr (chapter 2) examines the emergence of nationalism in the context of the changing international political order, as handled by an exceedingly perceptive thinker, who however was more interested in the international state system than in nationalism as such. For him, nationalism was the new *content*, whilst he was concerned with the *form*. Then there is a group of anti-nationalists: Julien Benda, who postulates, but does not really establish, a metaphysic which would be opposed to particularisms, whether national or other (chapter 4); Conor Cruise O'Brien, whose error is to take nationalism for granted as the primary and general social bond, and who then concerns himself with musing on how it can best be restrained from excessive, religiously inspired enthusiasm (chapter 5); Bronislaw Malinowski, who in effect found and commended a solution, namely a combination of cultural nationalism and political internationalism which he had seen practised in Cracow by the Habsburgs and in Africa by the British (chapter 6); Andrei Sakharov, who in fact practised an admirable universalism, and yet in his youth succumbed, in part, not to nationalism, but to an ethic and metaphysic of development (chapter 8). There is also Jan Patočka, whose alternative to modern ethnic/linguistic nationalism is not so much universalism on its own, but an older form of hierarchical and territorial patriotism, which however

paid its moral dues to universalism (chapter 10), and Václav
Havel, who faced the same enemy as Sakharov, but turned less
to science than to a kind of humanist suspicion of science (chapter 9).

Then there are the nationalists. Masaryk strove to combine
universalism with nationalism: his nationalism, and the revolution he effected on its behalf, were only legitimated in his eyes,
by the fact that they implemented a wider, universal and moral
movement of human history (chapter 9). Kemalism effected one
of the rare, perhaps the only, instance of a genuine nationalism
within the Muslim world that was not blended with religious
fundamentalism but, on the contrary, was opposed to it (chapter
7). Elsewhere in Islam, the high culture with which men identify,
when torn from their previous stable system of social niches, is
articulated in religious rather than in ethnic/national terms. The
great merit of Kemalism, and the blessing it conferred on Turkey,
lies in its nebulous rather than specific developmentalism: unlike
Leninism, it did not commit the country on which it was imposed to a definite and, in the event, disastrous socio-economic
programme. On the other hand, it is not clear whether it can
contain the strong current of religious revivalism. There is Edward
Said, who provided the rationale, not so much for any one
nationalism (not even the one with which he identifies himself),
as an omnibus charter for all nationalisms struggling against imperialism (chapter 12). Where Benda repudiated all particularistic
totem poles, national or imperial, in the name of a universalist
objective truth (the foundations of which he failed to work out),
Said's anti-imperialism invokes a similarly ill-founded social subjectivism: truth is granted to those born into the right camp, plus
those who politically choose to support them, but it is derisively
denied to those linked to empires. They are damned by what
they *are*. There is Heidegger, like Patočka endowed with a pheno-
menological philosophical background, not exactly a promising
foundation for nationalism: his nationalism seems opportunist
and unilluminating (chapter 11).

It is obvious that the complexity of the line-ups is almost
endless. Universalist transcendentalism, allowing the human mind

access to independent verities, if only it frees itself from local social shackles, competes with an insistence that truth can be found only through a return to a social womb; religion can appear as the alternative to nationalism, or, on the contrary, as that which over-excites nationalism and makes it intolerable (and intolerant); economic development is the motive or the great enemy of nationalism; traditionalism is the ally or the rival of ethnicity.

The aim of these essays is to explore and illuminate this variety of alignments. But the essays also appear at a moment when national turbulence is, once again, exceedingly prominent. The general pattern seems clear. Nationalism is like gravity, an important and pervasive force, but not, at *most* times, strong enough to be violently disruptive. The *ancien régimes* in Eastern Europe had, all in all, contained it, without excessive difficulty, until 1918. It was above all with the collapse of the poly-ethnic empire once linked to, but now no longer sustained by, the Counter-Reformation, that nationalism really erupted. It then created a system in its own image, which in the event proved so feeble as to lead to the domination of Eastern Europe by Hitler and Stalin.

The collapse of the second, and this time secular ideocracy, in 1989/91 has led to a very similar situation. It may in the end lead to a similar catastrophe. History does not repeat itself with precision or at all, and there is room for hope, or at least for the avoidance of dogmatic pessimism. But we must note the similarity of the elements in the situation: economic collapse, political disintegration, inflation and consequent wiping out of savings, emergence of opportunist and resented new wealth, national humiliation, the transformation of large proportions of the previously dominant cultural group into minorities in new national units, moral disorientation, facile and opportunist centrifugal nationalism . . .

So much for the bad news. But the world has changed. This second great post-imperial eruption of nationalism takes place in a different and new ideological climate, one in which the old link between territory and wealth has been broken, and the new political supremacy of growth-rates established, and one in which

Left and Right extremism has lost much of its conviction and repute. Notwithstanding the fact that the collapse of the secular communist ideocracy was provoked by relative economic decline, in absolute terms the situation is better than it was some generations ago, and men have more to lose.

So nationalism has lost none of its importance, but is operating in, so to speak, the context of a new constellation of ideas. These essays endeavour to contribute to an understanding of that new intellectual ambiance.

Ernest Gellner
Prague, Centre for the Study of Nationalism

Acknowledgements

These essays constitute the spin-off of sustained work on nationalism. I am grateful for financial support for this work both from the ESRC, thanks to a grant awarded on the initiative of the then Chairman, Sir Douglas Hague, and from the Nuffield Foundation, thanks to the support of the Assistant Director, Patricia Thomas.

The work was carried out initially whilst I was still a member of the Social Anthropology Department in the University of Cambridge. Many people in that department deserve my gratitude, but I should express particular thanks to Mrs Mary McGinley, Mrs Margaret Story and Mr Humphrey Hinton. Jack Messenger has been an admirable and patient editor.

The work was completed whilst at the Central European University in Prague. There, once again, the number of people who helped me is too large to enumerate, but some – fellow teachers, secretaries or patrons of the new university – deserve special mention for help and support: Vlasta Hirtová, Leila McAllister, Robin Cassling, Mark Griffin, Sukumar Periwal, Charles Bonner; Claire Wallace, Jiři Musil, Petr Pithart, Jitka Malečková, Guido Franzinetti, Alfred Stepan, Anne Lonsdale and George Soros.

The hope is that these essays make some contribution to the understanding of the problems with which the Centre for the Study of Nationalism is concerned.

Chapter 1 was first published in 1990 as 'The dramatis personae of history', a review of Roman Szporluk's, *Communism and Nationalism: Karl Marx versus Friedrich List, East European Politics and Societies*, vol. 4, no. 1, pp. 116–33. Chapter 2 was first published in 1992 as 'Nationalism reconsidered and E. H. Carr', *Review of International Studies*, vol. 18, pp. 285–93. Chapter 3 first appeared in 1989 in the USSR in *Novaia i Novieishiya Istoria*, no. 5, and in 1992 in B. Jewsiewicki and J. Létourneau (eds), *Constructions identitaires: questionnements théoriques et études de ces*, Quebec City: Laval University, *Actes du Célat*, May, pp. 63–72. Chapter 4 was first published in 1990 as 'La trahison de la trahison des clercs', in Ian Maclean, Alan Montefiore and Peter Winch (eds), *The Political Responsibility of Intellectuals*, Cambridge: Cambridge University Press, pp. 17–27. Chapter 5 was first published in 1989 as 'The sacred and the national', an essay review of Conor Cruise O'Brien, *Godland: Reflections on Religion and Nationalism*, *LSE Quarterly*, vol. 3, no. 4, winter, pp. 357–69. Chapter 6 was first published in 1987 as 'The political thought of Bronislaw Malinowski', *Current Anthropology*, vol. 28, no. 4, August-October, pp. 557–9. Chapter 7 was previously published in *When History Accelerates*, essays dedicated to Paul Stirling, edited by Chris Hann, Athlone Press, 1994. Chapter 8 was first published in 1990 as 'A reformer of the modern world', a review essay on Andrei Sakharov, *Memoirs*, in *Times Literary Supplement*, no. 4,559, 17–23 August, pp. 863–4. Chapter 9 originally appeared in a shortened version in the *Guardian*, 25 July 1992. It also appeared in full in *Telos, Quarterly Journal of Critical Thought*, no. 94, winter 1993/94, and in the *Budapest Review of Books*, vol. 2, no. 4, winter 1992, and also in the Hungarian version of the same journal. Chapter 10 first appeared in 1993 as 'Reborn from below: The forgotten beginnings of the Czech national revival', a review of Jan Patočka, *Co Jsou Češi? Was Sind die Tschechen?*, *Times Literary Supplement*, no. 4,702, 14 May, pp. 3–5. Chapter 11 was first published in 1993 as 'Mind games', a review of Hugo Ott, *Martin Heidegger: A Political Life* and Hans Sluga, *Heidegger's Crisis: Philosophy and Politics in Nazi Germany*, in *New Republic*, vol. 209, no. 21 (#4,114), 22 November, pp. 35–9. Chapter 12 was first published in 1993 as 'The mightier pen? Edward Said and the double standards of inside-out colonialism' (on Edward Said,

Culture and Imperialism), *Times Literary Supplement*, no. 4,690, 19 February, pp. 3–4. Chapter 13 was first published in 1992 as 'From the ruins of the great contest', *Times Literary Supplement*, no. 4,641, 17 March, pp. 9–10. Chapter 14 first appeared in Russian in *Put'* ('The Way'), no. 1, 1992, and also in Italian in 1993 as 'Il mito della nazione e quello delle classe', in P. Anderson, M. Aymard, P. Bairoch, W. Barberis, C. Ginzburg and G. Einaudi (eds), *Stori d'Europe*, vol. 1, *L'Europa Oggi*, Turin: Editore Guilio Einaudi, pp. 638–9.

Ernest Gellner
Centre for the Study of Nationalism
Central European University, Prague

1

Nationalism and Marxism

Around the turn of the eighteenth and nineteenth centuries, it became obvious that West European society was undergoing radical, structural change. It was radical in that the fundamental principles of organization were changing, and in that the very spirit of men was being transformed. Such change is totally unlike mere rotation of personnel within a more or less stable structure, or changes in structure which merely amount to a bit more of this and a bit less of that. The transformation was far more fundamental. It was also of more than merely local and temporary significance. It revealed what man really was and could be. It seemed to be the highly conspicuous and illuminating culmination of a long and pointed story. The message had not been visible to earlier generations; now it acquired a high profile. The story was endowed with a plot, and one which bode well for mankind as a whole. All in all, things were getting better, and would continue to do so. The idea of Progress was born.

At the same time, under the impact of philosophic and scientific ideas disseminated by the Enlightenment, religious belief was becoming intellectually ever more difficult to sustain. The conjunction of these two themes – loss of faith in a transcendent and personal God, and the acquisition of faith in a happy earthly destiny – inevitably blended and almost irresistibly pointed to an obvious solution: if God was not available, but pervasive Progress was, could not Progress deputize for God?

The idea, which seemed manifest and persuasive, found its most influential expression in the philosophy of Hegel. This thinker combined a fine metaphysical sweep and historical suggestiveness with impenetrably obscure and ambiguous prose. This had the inestimable advantage of failing to make clear whether the guiding spirit of history was replacing the God of Abraham, or was merely a continuation of the same deity under another name. Readers could suit themselves, and choose an interpretation consonant with their temperament, position or mood. The ambiguity of the position was part and parcel of its essence and its appeal.

There are countless questions that arise about the new vision. One is fundamental: what exactly are the units or sub-units in terms of which the structural transformations of human society are to be characterized? Structural change of human society means, if it means anything, some basic alteration in the relationship of the parts or elements of which mankind is composed. The dramatis personae of history change their positions relative to each other. But who or what exactly are those dramatis personae? This question is the subject of a remarkable study in the history of ideas, Roman Szporluk's *Communism and Nationalism: Karl Marx versus Friedrich List.*[1]

There are two principal candidates for the crucial role: classes and nations. Marxism notoriously opts for the former. If one were allowed but one sentence to define the central intuition of Marxism, one would naturally choose the famous sentence from the *Communist Manifesto*: All history of all hitherto existing society is the history of class struggles.

What does it mean to say that human society is universally pervaded by class struggle? On the surface, it is not remotely true. Visible conflict between social strata does indeed occur in some places, for instance in the course of plebeian, peasant or slave uprisings, but just as frequently, it is absent. In many societies and at many times, diverse strata accept their station and

---

[1]   Roman Szporluk, *Communism and Nationalism: Karl Marx versus Friedrich List* (New York, Oxford: Oxford University Press, 1988).

its duties, and there is at least no manifest and visible conflict between them. Lateral conflict between stratified neighbouring societies, where the strata fight not for themselves but for the geographic unit of which they are part, are much more common. The Marxist counter-affirmation that class conflict is nevertheless latent, similar to Hobbes' claim that states are ever at war with each other, even when they are not, seems to have the following concrete, empirical content: contrary to a variety of mollifying ideologies, the actual class structure is neither stable, nor permanent, nor genuinely in the interests of all the parties concerned. There is nothing to enforce or guarantee it permanently. The class structure only reflects the current and unstable, transitory condition of the forces of production. But the state of the forces of production will not remain as it now is. Hence the class structure itself will also not remain stable. Neither is there a need, let alone any justification, for the participants to treat it as such. Hostilities are bound to re-open, and only false consciousness misrepresents an informal truce as a permanent human and social condition. Change is the law of all things, and the essence of social change is the transformation of class structures. The inherent instability of class relations means that the occupants of diverse social positions will not merely have the opportunity, but also the inescapable destiny, of eventually seeing them changed. They owe no loyalty to their station and its duties. The system of stations is undergoing ineluctable change, and it is only the final unstructured classless destination, and not the current status quo with its spurious air of permanence, which can claim our enlightened and justified allegiance.

If social stability were a fact or even a genuine possibility, the affirmation that latent conflict lurks under the façade of harmony or accommodation would become a somewhat empty and quasi-metaphysical claim. If, as many right-wing people believe, the need for stratification is inherent in human nature, the stress on conflicts of interest could only alert men to the possibility of a rotation of personnel in the social hierarchy. It would still be possible for the first to be last, and the last to be first, but it would not be possible to abolish the division of society into those who are first and those who are last. It is the affirmation of the possibility of radically changing the kind of stratification and of abolishing it altogether, which endows the relatively trivial – because obvious – perception that some social positions are more attractive than others with a really interesting and novel content. The cutting edge and content of the affirmation of the perennial presence of the class conflict is not the truism that social positions are differentiated and that some are more advantageous than others, but the untrivial perception that the system of positions is unstable and bound to change – plus the very highly contentious idea that it is possible, or ultimately inevitable, for mankind to manage without any such system at all. The important Marxist claim is not that men occupy very diverse social roles, but the novel claim that those who occupy fixed and unequal positions are in conflict with each other, even if they know it not. The contingent nature of stratification is underscored by a sociological theory that links it to the state of the forces of production, and the claim that at a certain level of development of those forces, stratification is neither necessary nor possible. The Marxist affirmation of the unappeasable nature of class conflict contains the denial of two harmony doctrines, pervasively influential at the time that Marxism was born: the liberal doctrine that the hidden hand of the free market operates in everyone's favour, and the conservative doctrine that a peace-keeping state maintains the balance even-handedly, in the interest of all the constituent parts of society.

What is more, in this formulation, much of what is said seems valid. Without necessarily accepting specific Marxist doctrines, still less the doctrine that a genuinely classless society is feasible, it is indisputably true that no particular class structure is permanent, and that the way in which society divides its members into sub-groups is indeed subject to radical change. It is in no way inscribed into the eternal nature and order of things. There is no valid ideological justification for any one social order, and no one balance of power underlying a given order is permanent. It is still possible to find conservatives who maintain that inequality is justified simply because it is inevitable; possibly so, but the forms of inequality are legion. They vary a great deal, and the variety is a legitimate object both of scholarly curiosity and of political manipulation. We are not destined to endure any single one of them, even if we cannot escape all of them.

This much, then, is shared ground: social structure is a variable and not a datum. It is neither fixed nor normative. But it does not in any way follow from this that the really crucial opposition, which constitutes the key to understanding historic change, is conflict between classes, rather than human subdivisions of some other kind. It is anything but self-evident. Under the impact of Darwinism, for instance, the idea that history is the story of struggle between genetically distinct populations, some better endowed than others, once again became fashionable and politically influential.

This is the backbone of Szporluk's book: given that history is a process in which the relationships of sub-groups or sub-populations to each other do change, exactly which sub-groups are to be selected as crucial? Which memberships, which loyalty really matters? Why classes rather than nations?

For Marxism, the role of human sub-groups arises at two quite distinct levels. These might be called the Social Metaphysics and the Historical Sociology of Marxism. Szporluk's book is very interesting about the social metaphysics of Marxism. Intermediate human classifications – religious, political or ethnic – standing between man and humanity at large, all constitute forms of undesirable alienation. Szporluk quotes from a statement of Engels made in 1847:

The nationalities of the people who joined together . . . will be . . . compelled by this union to merge with one another and thereby supersede themselves as the various differences between estates and classes disappear through the superseding of their basis – private property.

Unambiguously, the future was to be nationless as well as classless and religionless. The social metaphysic of Marx and Engels is a very curious mixture of individualist anarchism and a pan-human communalism. National divisions by class and religion are ultimately spurious and constitute obstacles preventing man from realizing his species-being, wherein his true fulfilment lies. His real destiny is to be free of the constraints imposed on him by his membership in class, ethnic or religious categories, and indeed by any social roles. At the same time he will somehow be automatically incorporated in a harmonious universal community. The precise nature of the hidden hand which is to perform this latter miracle was not elaborated by the founding fathers of Marxism.

So there are, as it were, two levels of spuriousness, radically different in their significance. Nations and classes are equally excluded from the true human essence, and together with religion, are destined for extinction. But whilst all such alienating, intermediate constraining categorizations of man are spurious, some are more spurious than others. Class may ultimately be philosophically spurious: but it is not historically or sociologically spurious. Anything but. History is the history of *class* struggle. It is not, or only superficially, the history of *national* struggles.

In order to understand both the mechanics of human alienation and those of human liberation, we need to analyse it in class terms. Amongst all the ultimately spurious divisions of mankind, class nevertheless has a special causal efficacy, both in the production of alienating social relations, and in the eventual liberation. It constitutes an obstacle to our fulfilment, and it is an important, weighty obstacle. The other categorizations, ethnic or religious for instance, are indeed obstacles, but in themselves are not very important. They are merely superficial manifestations of the real hindrances to the consummation of history. Class is noxious, but historically relevant. The other categorizations suffer from the double indignity of being both noxious and unimportant. And it is the proletariat, as a very special class, in but not of civil society, which will liberate mankind from class-endowed society altogether.

The Marxist mistakes in social metaphysics and in sociology converge on what of course is the single most crucial and disastrous error in the system. The supposition that the communist social order will require no political organization but will in some unexplained way be self-adjusting, that it will be guided, in an even more powerful and mysterious form, by that hidden hand which the liberals in their more modest way attributed only to a well-insulated economic sphere – all that follows both from the metaphysical dismissal of all human sub-categorizations in general, and from the more immediate sociological exclusion of ethnic and political ones from the effective causal machinery of social change and stability. The sad consequence is that societies living 'under the banner of Marxism' are simply deprived of any idiom in which even to discuss their political predicament. If power relations, as distinct from class relations, are irrelevant or will disappear, there is no need, indeed there is no warrant, for codifying their proper and legitimate limits and deployment. The Kingdom of God needs no constitutional law. If, on the other hand, politics are in fact indispensable under any form of human organization, and if the human species-essence possesses none of the miraculous capacities for fulfilment in harmonious, or at least non-antagonistic work, with which Marx credited it, then we are in trouble. The same is true if ethnicity is similarly indispensable. Marxist societies do in fact discuss the 'national question', but are greatly constrained ideologically in what they can say about it. As for the political form of communist society, they cannot really discuss it at all.

The main question to which Szporluk specially addresses himself, and for the discussion of which he invokes Friedrich List, is not the overall, metaphysical irrelevance of all human sub-classifications. It is the more specific and immediate dismissal of ethnic and ethnic–political ones from the account of historical development. Here he claims not merely that List was right and Marx wrong, but also that latter-day Marxists have unwittingly become crypto-Listians. Under Marxist terminology, look out for *listig* practices, to use Marx's pun (*listig* = cunning).

Why was it that Marx and Engels chose classes rather than nations as the subdivisions of mankind in terms of which the true plot of history was to be mapped out? One can think of a number of obvious reasons:

1   It was a corollary of their social metaphysics in which the
    proletariat was a special class, liberated by its distinctive con-
    dition from allegiance to all and every alienating sub-group
    identification. Hence it was destined to be the carrier, the
    embodiment, as well as the agent of universal human libera-
    tion, of the emergence of the true human species-being. It is
    not clear how a social metaphysic postulating nations as the
    building blocks of mankind could plausibly single out any
    one nation as the liberator of all the others. A class whose
    members are by their very social position deprived of and
    liberated from the constraints that the social order otherwise
    imposes on men, could reasonably be singled out for the
    special role of saviour, without introducing an offensively
    arbitrary asymmetry into the system.

2   Product differentiation. Inter-polity and inter-ethnic conflict
    was a commonplace. Everyone knew it took place. Conven-
    tional historiography was preoccupied with it almost to the
    exclusion of all else; it has been taking place for a very long
    time and one could hardly claim any originality if one stressed
    it. Such a claim could not possibly be presented as the un-
    masking of a hitherto hidden, latent meaning of history.

3   The sheer fact that conflict between political units and, some-
    times, between ethnic groups, has been going on for so long
    made it hard to invoke as the explanation of the new and
    dramatic structural changes in West European societies. Some
    of these changes, notably the industrial revolution in Eng-
    land, were in the main internal to single polities, and not
    primarily connected with inter-political or inter-ethnic con-
    flicts. The basic transformations accompanying the first in-
    dustrial revolution manifested themselves as changes in the
    class structure, not in ethnic structure. Class relations and
    their changes were more plausible candidates for the dramatis
    personae of current history at least. Marx and Engels then
    extrapolated and concluded that they also had been the real
    underlying factors responsible for the slower and less visible

structural changes of the past. Only class conflict could explain current change, and if all historical change was to be
explained by a single principle, then this had better be it.
Inter-ethnic or inter-political conflict was merely the conspicuous but irrelevant froth on the surface. The outcome of
such conflicts presumably only determined the identity of the
personnel occupying diverse positions (e.g. the identities of
masters and slaves, of lords and serfs). It did not affect the
social structures themselves.

On the basis of the evidence available and conspicuous in the
early nineteenth century, the Marxist conclusion is certainly
reasonable. The view that the industrial revolution was the most
important thing that was happening at the time was eminently
sensible. There is no obvious logical link between the industrial
revolution and inter-ethnic conflict. It is possible to claim that
English loot from India played a part in the industrial revolution,
but it would be absurd to claim it as *the* cause. The English were
not the only conquerors to loot India, and the other conquerors
did not use the loot to fuel industrial development. As for the
fine English record in the eighteenth-century wars with France –
the score was 4:1 – it reflected rather than caused English economic development.

If thereupon, in the Hegelian spirit, one is to seek a single
overall key to history, it is natural to conclude that earlier structural changes had also been constituted by intra-social transformations of the relations between strata, rather than by inter-polity
or inter-ethnic conflict. The inference has a certain plausibility.
It is not at all clear why the ethnic identity of occupants of
diverse social positions should make much difference to the system
as such, in other words to the class structure. By contrast, the
supposition that the kind of structure that is imposed on society
is determined by the available forces of production has great
appeal and plausibility. For various reasons it is not fully cogent.
For instance, there is no guarantee that the underlying mechanism of social change is similar in all the great historic transformations. Nor is it obvious (or indeed true) that the available forces

of production uniquely determine the class structure of the society dependent on those forces. But, cogent or not, the central Marxist intuition about the deep structure of historical change had enormous plausibility. In the light of the industrial revolution the view that classes, not nations, are the real dramatis personae of history is exceedingly natural and persuasive. If it is in error, the story of its rectification deserves to be told, and Szporluk's book does it.

Szporluk's main claim on behalf of his hero List is that he was the first to perceive clearly that the central Marxist intuition, notwithstanding its inherent plausibility in the light of the industrial revolution, was misguided. List is credited by Szporluk with at least two distinct perceptions:

1   A social ontology that makes nations the eternal and legitimate subdivision of mankind. 'For List,' says Szporluk, 'the division of humanity into nations was the central truth.' He quotes List as affirming that 'between each individual and entire humanity . . . stands the NATION' (p. 115). 'On the nature of *nationality*, as the intermediate interest between those of *individualism* and of *entire humanity*, my whole structure is based.'
2   A more specific sociological doctrine concerning the diffusion of the benefits of industrialism, which confers a special importance on ethnic groups in this process.

Szporluk's expositions of List very convincingly make it appear that for List, at any rate, (1) is an essential premise for (2). The distinction between the two levels corresponds roughly to the distinction in Marxism between what I called its social metaphysics, the ultimate irrelevance or illegitimacy of *all* human subdivisions, and its sociology, the irrelevance of nations contrasted with classes, for the purpose of understanding the mechanics of 'prehistory' and the social condition in which we are still enmeshed.

Now it seems to me that in so far as List does indeed treat (1) as a necessary premise for (2), he is misguided. Hence Szporluk's evaluation of List is over-generous. It fails to chide him for this mistake. The evidence offered by Szporluk on this point is somewhat ambiguous. On the one hand, Szporluk quotes List as pronouncing that nations are 'eternal' (*sic*). He also observes that '[m]odern, that is, political (and not only linguistic), nations for List were a relatively recent phenomenon.' This rather leaves it open for one to credit List with the view that the kind of nations characteristic of the nineteenth century were not eternal after all, but were engendered by the process of diffusion of industrialism which concerned List. With such an interpretation, (1) ceases to be an indispensable and relevant premise. It is the *kind* of nation engendered by recent industrialism, or the shadow cast by its coming, that is relevant for understanding the diffusion of the new industrial order. If this is so, we can dispense with nations as the alleged 'eternal' accompaniments of social life. The nature of industrialism contains all the premisses we need, and the eternity of nations does not concern us one way or the other. This happens to be my view of the matter. My own guess would be that List was less than clear in his own mind whether or not he really needed (1) in order to establish (2). My own belief is that (1) is neither true in itself, nor necessary as a premise for List's perfectly valid conclusions concerning the diffusion of industrialism, and that List's failure to be clear on this point constitutes a weakness in his thought.

The point of overlap between List and the founding fathers of Marxism is their shared perception of the invalidity of the legitimating ideology of the new industrial order, i.e. of the *laissez-faire* doctrine of free trade. According to this doctrine, unrestrained economic competition is eventually beneficial to everyone. The flaw in the argument is that those who enter the free market do not do so on equal terms. Some are constrained by their weakness to accept unfavourable terms. List's rejection of optimistic liberalism, which would turn all mankind into beneficiaries of the free market, is somewhat more ambivalent and restrained than that of the Marxists. Initially List questioned the doctrine because it would work only if all participating units observed the rules. Since some in fact fail to do so, the others need to protect themselves against such free or early riders.

But he moved on to a more radical repudiation of a generalized economic liberalism, based on the need to protect late developers. The Marxist rejection of the liberal model is of course inspired by the conviction that unequal terms were not a contingent flaw, but an inherent and necessary feature of the system: even if there were no inequality of strength at the start (though there was), the sheer natural workings of the system would eventually ensure its appearance and its aggravation. There was for him no special need to protect late developers, since their suffering would be no worse than that of the victims of early, and hence all the more painfully protracted, development of capitalism.

This is one of the crucial points in the argument: the role of the state as an essential, indispensable protector of late economic developers. It is here that early Marxism confronted List, in the *Communist Manifesto*. Contrary to the widespread view that Marxism simply underestimated and hence largely ignored nationalism, Szporluk maintains that an important section of the manifesto is devoted to an implicit onslaught on and polemic with List, and that only Harold Laski had actually noticed this. 'If Laski is right,' Szporluk says, 'the *Communist Manifesto* is . . . also an "antinationalist manifesto" by someone who had confronted German nationalism through the works of its main spokesman – Friedrich List' (p. 62).

Marx had not only learned about nationalist theory from List. Ironically, as Szporluk stresses, it was through this nationalist critic of cosmopolitan liberalism that Marx first learned about *laissez-faire* economics. He had been initiated into the teaching of that school by a rival fellow-critic, whom however he also heartily despised. List, according to Marx, 'despite all his boasting . . . has put forward *not a single proposition* that had not been advanced long before him. . . . Only the illusions and idealizing language . . . belong to Herr List' (p. 39). For Marx, List was simply repeating arguments initially propounded in defence of the Napoleonic Continental System. As Szporluk observes:

So much for the cause of national unification and economic modernization of Germany – some practical results of which Marx would live long enough to see with his own eyes. (p. 39)

This is the heart of the matter: the relation between nationalism and industrialization. Szporluk's message is: Marx got it wrong, and List got it right. Moreover, latter-day Marxists are really crypto-Listians. Marxism was used to protect late industrializers by providing them with a national–political shell.

Marx expressed himself in favour of free trade with contemptuous irony, because it 'breaks up old nationalities and carries antagonism of proletariat and bourgeoisie to the uttermost point. In a word, the Free Trade system hastens the Social Revolution. In this revolutionary sense alone . . . I am in favour of Free Trade' (p. 41). He was quite clear about nationalism:

> The nationality of the worker is neither French, nor English, nor German, it is *labor*. . . . His government is neither French, nor English, nor German, it is *capital*. His native air is neither French, nor German, nor English, it is *factory air*. (p. 35)

Marx did see that the protectionism commended by List was intended to enable the German bourgeoisie to develop its own 'national road to capitalism' (Szporluk's phrase): that much is common ground. Where they differed was that he did not think they had any chance of succeeding. Free trade internally, protectionism outwardly he held to be a contradiction, and the idea of nationalism was simply the smokescreen intended to hide the absurdity of it all from those who propounded it.

In the event, the alleged absurdity turned out to be the crucial reality of the nineteenth and twentieth centuries. It was both feasible and terrifyingly effective. Worse still: the actual role of Marxism in the form in which it actually came to be implemented in the real world, was Listian. The national road to either capitalism or socialism was not only viable, but mandatory. It was the *national* path to industrialism that was essential. Capitalism and socialism are single variants of it – though one may add that capitalism seems considerably more efficient, and commits the society undergoing it to far less false consciousness concerning its own organization, than does socialism.

Szporluk is interesting on Marx's view of national backwardness.

Germany was in Marx's view a curious case, an anachronism: an overturning of the established order in Germany in 1843 would hardly bring the country up to the French level of 1789. In philosophy, on the other hand, Germany was altogether up to date, if not ahead of its time. Marx had his own and Engels' ideas in mind. This backwardness and uneven development, according to Szporluk's exegesis of Marx, could not be corrected by economic insulation intended to enable German economic–political development to catch up; on the contrary, it was to be overcome by stage-jumping, effected by the submersion of German history in universal history. The non-national liberating class was just becoming ready even in Germany, though the signal for the revolution was to come from France. It was the German bourgeoisie and its ideologue List who were misguided in wishing to propel Germany through what were later to become the canonical Marxist historical stages, at any rate as far as the capitalist stage, by striving for capitalism-in-a-single-country and by using the spurious idea of nationalism for so doing. A sociological chimera was being propounded in the name of a spurious patriotism, or so Marx thought.

All this does of course throw fascinating light, as Szporluk notes, on what was later to happen in Russia.

> Marx did not admit the possibility of a national road to capitalism
> . . . and had nothing to say in favor of socialism in one country,
> because capitalism and communism were worldwide systems and
> could be treated only in a supranational setting.

So the whole problem of explaining how a revolution could occur in a backward country did not really arise. There was only a world-system, and national boundaries were not of any profound importance. So the Russians need not have worried, and, as Szporluk says, they could have 'saved themselves this argument, but only if they had first given up their concern for Russia and thought of themselves as members of the entire human race'. Mind you, in the 1840s Marx held the Russians, as Szporluk points out, to be excluded from the world-historical process altogether.

By the end of the century they were presumably included, as much as the Germans had been in the 1840s.

If Szporluk's account of Marx is correct, and it is certainly persuasive, then it is incumbent upon me to withdraw certain criticisms I have directed at the outstanding contemporary Soviet Marxist theoretician Yuri Semenov.[2] Semenov has tried to rehabilitate the Marxist notion of socio-economic formations and the associated conception of historic stages, and by implication to remove the puzzle concerning the occurrence of a communist revolution in backward Russia, by claiming that formations or stages applied not to individual nations, but only to the global history of all mankind. It was never really intended to apply to single societies, and so the question addressed to Marxists – why are certain stages missing in the fates of this or that society – is inherently misguided. My comment was that the resulting theory was indeed ingenious and interesting, but not faithful to the spirit and intention of the Marxism of the founding fathers.[3] It was, on the other hand, very well suited to the then ideological needs of the contemporary Soviet Union. It provided a theoretical charter for the idea of historic leadership: if global stages were determined by the social form prevalent in the leading society, then the socialist stage needs a leader as much as any other, and (as is implied though not actually stated), what society better suited to exercise such leadership than the Soviet Union?

If Szporluk is right, a similar basic idea was already just as conspicuously present in Marx's thought in the 1840s, though no doubt for other reasons. It was Listian nationalism, not Marxism, which thought in terms of parallel but unsynchronized development. It was precisely the Marxist insistence on a single, unique world history that separated the two. The difference between Marx and Semenov then becomes one only of detail: Marx thought that it would be the blending of up-to-date (or

[2]   Yuri Semenov, 'Theory of socio-economic formations and world history' in E. Gellner, ed., *Soviet and Western Anthropology* (London, 1980).
[3]   Ernest Gellner, 'A Russian Marxist philosophy of history' in E. Gellner, ed., *Soviet and Western Anthropology* (London, 1980).

ahead-of-time) German philosophy, i.e. his own, and a belated
German proletariat, with the economic and political development of England and France, that would bring about the crucial
revolution.

By contrast, Semenov, writing 'at dusk', after history had
revealed its design, can record the fact that the external late-
coming catalyst was not Germany but Russia. But the young
Marx evidently believed that latecomers not merely need not,
but indeed could not, pass through capitalism in its full and
protracted form. Had he persisted in such a view, his replies to
Vera Zasulich could have been more confident and less tentative.
In fairness to Semenov, it must be said that his argument at this
point remains abstract and does not actually name the country
involved in the peripheral transition to socialism. He contents
himself with pointing out the essential role of a backward periphery in leading mankind to a higher stage, noting that this had
also been the pattern in the emergence of a slave society and of
feudalism. Hence the periphery is crucial, not marginal, to historic change. Only capitalism, very eccentric in this respect, had
emerged endogenously.

If Marx was wrong, in what senses and to what extent did List
get it right? The first thing to note about List is that he was a
nationalist, but not a romantic. He welcomed, and did not repudiate, the industrial revolution. The nation was to be protected
not by insulating it from industrialism, but on the contrary, by
adopting and mastering it. Romanticism noted the disruptive
character of industrialism and capitalism, as did Marx, but re-
acted against it by proposing to keep it out. Marx thought it
neither could nor should be kept out, but that on the far side of
the havoc it wrought there lay a new and beneficent order, a
Gemeinschaft of all mankind, blending individual freedom with
social harmony. (Why he confidently thought this, and allowed
himself irritable impatience with anyone refusing to share this
rosy optimism, passes all understanding.)

List was original in wishing neither to keep industrialism out
nor to submit to it, but to take it on by making it *national*. Not
national socialism, but national capitalism was his aim.

This idea really contains two quite distinct components that must be separated:

1 The use of political institutions to protect and promote industrialization.
2 The requirement that these political institutions be ethnic ones.

Very fundamental questions hinge on this, concerning the relative roles of endogenous evolution and of lateral diffusion in historical transformation, and concerning the mechanisms of lateral change. Marxism is primarily endogenist–evolutionist, but ambivalently incorporates diffusionist elements, with questionable consistency. But the big question here is whether the agents of diffusion are a) political or b) ethnic, and what kind of ethnicity is involved. The correct answer seems to be *yes* to both; and as for the kind of ethnicity involved, the correct answer is – the educationally transmitted, literate shared-culture of the modern industrial state, and not the *Gemeinschaft*-transmitted, pre-Gutenberg communalism of old.

The two requirements are logically quite separate. The second in no way automatically follows from the first. They need to be considered in turn, and one needs to ask why List embraced both of them. The argument for (1), in rough outline, is that without political aid and protection, industrial development in backward areas either does not take place at all, or has intolerably disruptive and uneven effects. It favours some but depresses many others, and the losers probably outnumber those who gain. Its social side-effects are liable to be specially catastrophic.

But if all this be admitted, why should the political institution, the centralized state, presiding over the development of a backward area, necessarily be a national one? What are the arguments for (2)? Why should it not be a non-national empire, such as that of the Habsburgs or the Ottomans? In fact, the Habsburg empire, or rather parts of it, did quite well industrially for a time. It is hard to see how the Ottoman empire could have done it: its ethos separated rulers and producers, by virtue of the principle expressed in the famous Circle of Equity, which claimed that rulers should keep the peace, that the ruled should sustain the rulers by producing a surplus, and that the two should not meddle in each other's affairs.[4] The rulers were reluctant to soil themselves with production, or indeed to tolerate the enhanced wealth, power and status of the producers, which would have inevitably followed on successful development. The ethnic distinctiveness, territorial discontinuity and religious stigma of the most effective producers made it hard for them to co-operate with the rulers in the intimate, production-oriented manner required by modernization-from-above. But leaving aside the distinctive ethos of the Ottomans, it is not immediately clear why the developmental state, a protector of industry not of faith, had to be a national one. I believe that this is indeed so, but the reasons are not self-evident, and the interesting question is – did List understand them? He saw that nationalism had to be economic; but did he also see that and why politically guided development had to be national?

I see no evidence in Szporluk's book that List properly understood the connection. Szporluk goes out of his way to provide List with a theory he might have held, had he formulated it in Hegelian–Marxist language: the nation 'in itself' was a 'permanent fixture of history' (Szporluk's phrase), but nations 'for themselves' were new, and List tried to help Germans to become one. To achieve this, a nation had to be a 'community with cultural, as well as political and economic forms of collective existence'. If 'culture' here means a shared High (i.e. literate, educationally transmitted) Culture, then this does indeed correspond to the modern industrial or industrializing nation. But the correct question seems to me not whether a nation must become such a nation-for-itself if it is to survive (as a nation) under conditions of industrialism, but the obverse: does a viable economic–political unit, capable of surviving in these conditions, also need to be a national one?

The nearest Szporluk comes to giving evidence that List saw this connection is when he quotes List's comments on Adam

[4]   See for instance Lucette Valensi, *Venise et la Sublime Porte* (Hachette, 1987).

Smith: 'For [Adam Smith] no *nation* exists, but merely a community, i.e. a number of individuals dwelling together' (p. 137). His comment on Adam Smith's ethno-blindness implies that he himself was sensitive to the ethnic role in the growth of the wealth of nations. List was enormously perceptive about a number of things crucial to the history of the nineteenth and twentieth centuries and of economic growth – the importance of the polity, of formal education and training, and of the administrative and cultural infrastructure of the economy. Knowledge, education, the cultural infrastructure and bureaucratic support all are crucial, and excessive concentration on labour and capital obscures it. Forging the political and cultural (hence eventually ethnic) framework is the key to late industrialism. The supposition that they will be dismantled, anticipated by Marxism, is the *real* chimera – and not ethnically defined protectionism, as Marx thought. In all this, List was superior to Marx, and much more prescient.

2

Nationalism and the International Order

E. H. Carr's *Nationalism and After*, which first appeared in 1945, receives little note in our recent discussions of nationalism. That it seems to have been forgotten is unjust; it is certainly wrong on my own part. I know that I read this book in my youth, and that I was greatly impressed by it. What however had impressed me at the time was a kind of general characteristic of the book and of the intellectual orientation of its author: the fact that it was clearly about the real world. I was not at all used to that.

I had been trained in Oxford, largely in economics and philosophy, and the relationship between the style of thought prevalent in each of these disciplines on the one hand and reality on the other was clouded in obscurity. Economic theory was largely deductive, and its premisses postulated individuals with clearly articulated, privately chosen ends, seeking to satisfy them in a world of limited means. I knew full well that such a condition, if it ever applied at all, certainly did not apply to all men at all times, but the question of delimiting the zone in which this kind of economic theory could operate was hardly asked by economists.

This essay is based on the eighth annual E. H. Carr Memorial Lecture delivered at the University College of Wales, Aberystwyth, in November 1991. E. H. Carr was Woodrow Wilson Professor of International Politics there from 1936 to 1947.

They seemed to think that it did apply to the parts of the world that mattered, and that the rest was a kind of ontological slum unworthy of attention.

If the economists thought that the world was more universally modern than in fact it was, then the philosophy which was emerging at that time, and which was being hailed as a great and final revelation, made exactly the opposite mistake: it claimed that the correct way to proceed in philosophy was by observing and accepting the conceptual customs of one's community, because such customs alone, enshrined in the habits of speech, could authorize our intellectual procedures. The fact that men had been systematically scrutinizing the customs of their own communities, at least in parts of Europe, for some four centuries or two millennia or longer, did not seem to interest them at all. If the economists were uncritical pan-modernists, the philosophers were becoming equally uncritical pan-romantics, though they did not so describe themselves.

That was the intellectual climate faced by a student of the famous Philosophy, Politics and Economics (PPE) course in Oxford. The fact that politics were also on the menu did not help matters much: it was, in fact, announced about that time that the subject was due to die pretty soon. As a matter of fact the same was also claimed for philosophy, but its death was somehow supposed to be specially glorious, a kind of Viking's funeral, and the illumination provided by this particular decease, was to confer special and remarkable benefits on mankind.

I was not terribly impressed by the conventional wisdom which was then taught and rather eagerly embraced by my contemporaries, but I lacked the confidence to repudiate and reject it with emphasis, at any rate at once. But the uneasy state of mind this engendered did at least make me receptive to someone who did not display the same faults as did advocates of the then current fashions. That is why Carr appealed to me. E. H. Carr's mind, as visible in his *Nationalism and After*, clearly was not guilty of that near-total insensitivity to the diversity of historical situations and context which otherwise prevailed in the academic world.

And yet he was, it seemed, a respected academic! I did not know at that time about the ambiguity of his position in the Establishment. But here was a man dealing with a phenomenon, nationalism, which I knew to be real and important, and dealing with it in a manner which was intelligible and which related it to major changes in society. I was very impressed, and the recollection of this stayed with me, but not any of the details of his arguments. In due course, I found my own way back to the real world, and later still, gave some attention to nationalism.[1]

I must have quite forgotten the details of Carr's book on the subject, for I did not go back to it and did not mention it or include it in my bibliography, yet my argument overlapped with his to quite a considerable extent, and I am open to the suspicion of theft. If theft there was, it was unconscious and unintended, but none the less it may well have occurred. It was only when the invitation to give the E. H. Carr Memorial Lecture led me to re-read him, that I realized I may have borrowed without acknowledgement and indeed without being aware of it. At the same time, the lecture and its publication provide an opportunity for making amends.

There is of course a difference in angle and approach. Carr was more interested in examining the state and the international order and in explaining why the nation or nationalism had captured them, than he was in the emergence of the nation as both a social unit and a kind of pre-eminent political norm. The questions overlap, but they are not identical. It becomes evident in his very first sentence, in which he endorses what he describes as the 'commonly assumed' view that nations in the modern sense emerged from the break-up of medieval Christendom. He goes on to qualify this common assumption by saying that the character of nations did not remain constant in this period. This may simply be his way of saying that nations in the modern sense only emerged later. Just how much is to be put into his words can perhaps become clear if we look at the periodicization which he immediately goes on to propose.

[1] Ernest Gellner, *Nations and Nationalism* (Oxford, 1983).

Stages in the Evolution of Nationalism

First, there is the post-medieval break-up, the replacement of a universal order by a system composed of sovereign states, and above all, their rulers. To me, this period would not seem to be nationalist at all; it was only such in the sense that the actors were sovereign and independent, and if 'nationalism' is the only alternative to 'inter-nationalism', then in that purely residual or negative sense, it was already a nationalist age. The most one could add is that some of the sovereign political units which operated at this time corresponded, in the composition of their populations, to what were later recognized to be nations. But is that enough to count this as a nationalist age? It seems to me preferable to work with a set of alternatives richer than the nationalist–internationalist opposition. What all this suggests is that Carr's primary concern was precisely with the balancing of particularistic and universalistic considerations, and nationalism in the narrower and more specific sense interested him mainly as something which strengthened particularism.

Carr's second period is one in which the sovereign states persist, but their content, so to speak, changes. States are no longer made up only of their rulers, or of their rulers plus the nobility. Just how much was to be included in the nation was contested or ambiguous, but clearly it was much extended. This development contained the seeds of a complete extension, embracing the entire population.

What it all amounts to in a way is this: an international moral order, based on a shared religious faith and its authoritative institutional incarnation, acting as arbiter of political propriety, has two contrasts rather than one. On the one hand, there is the fragmentation into fully sovereign political units, which as it were constitute, each of them, a moral apex not further accountable to anyone. There is on the other hand the doctrine that the ultimate repository of moral authority is the *nation*. These two alternatives to an international moral order appeared in succession in European history, and in some places, though in some only, the first prepared the ground for the second, though it failed to resemble it in important ways: the sovereign enlightened despots of the eighteenth century were neither national nor populist, but shared an international French High Culture. (It was by the standards of that culture that they were 'enlightened'.) But nationalism did not require this personal emancipation of monarchs as a precondition: on the contrary, it made its most dramatic impact in areas where this emancipation had not made itself felt. Though the Habsburgs had given up the pretence of being Holy Roman Emperors, the aura of a universal monarchy certainly clung to the Ottoman khalifate, and Moscow had its aspirations to being the Third Rome. Strictly speaking, Carr's theme is the fragmentation of a universal or international order, rather than nationalism as such: he sees nationalism as a special form which the fragmentation takes on, and specifies, very lucidly, why that form eventually emerged.

In Carr's view, the success of the system established in 1815 was due to a delicate balance between national and international interests: an international free-trade system, presented and accepted as the work of the Hidden Hand, was acceptable, largely because it engendered prosperity, and partly because the fact that the hand was invisible prevented many from noticing that it was not impersonal but British. 'The secrecy in which the activities of the city of London were veiled served to mask economic realities from those who thought in traditional political terms.'[2] Nationalism could be humane and liberal because nations, though they replaced rulers, remained clubs with restricted entry, free trade worked and engendered prosperity, and the links between polity and economy were decently obscured.

The third stage, in Carr's periodicization, begins to make its appearance about 1870 but develops fully after 1914. Here Carr invokes three factors: the expansion of the nation to include the lower orders, or, in other words, the healing of the breach between the 'two nations' which had characterized the earlier part of the century; the shift of attention to economic power; and finally, the diffusion of nationalism (or the conditions which engender

[2]   E. H. Carr, *Nationalism and After* (London, 1945), p.16.

it). 'The socialization of the nation has as its natural corollary the nationalization of socialism.'[3] Carr then proceeds to reflect on the '20th-century alliance between nationalism and socialism'. Carr also speculates on the possibility of a fourth stage, to follow the settlement of 1945.

If one looks at the history of Europe since the eighteenth century from the viewpoint of the emergence of nations and nationalism, rather than from that of the development of a state system, one does really get something rather similar to Carr's account, but from a different perspective, or in a different idiom. The multi-state community of sovereign polities in the eighteenth century, with their shared loyalty to a Crowned Heads' guild and its rules and etiquette, their professionalism and their tolerance of neutrals and non-combatants even amongst their own subjects, does not really belong to the age of nationalism at all. At most, one might be inclined to have the settlement of the Congress of Vienna included, since it was an attempt to re-establish a dynastic–religious order at a time when the forces destined to disrupt it had already made themselves felt.

The second stage would be that of Nationalist Irredentism, stretching from the first national uprisings in the course of the third decade of the nineteenth century, to the final triumph of the nationalist principle in 1918. Carr suggests that the old regime bribed its way to a temporary survival, in as far as the settlement of 1815 was followed by prosperity, something which those who had drawn it up could not have foreseen. But the prosperity was not just some kind of extraneous intrusion, even if it was, as Carr suggests, an unforeseen windfall for the rulers. It was the by-product of the same social changes which also, in his terms, socialized the nation. The society of perpetual economic growth was also one of occupational mobility, increasing technical sophistication in production (hence the need for universal education), and eventually widespread 'semanticization' of work, if the word may be allowed, i.e. turning work into the manipulation of meanings at the controls of a machine or in

---

[3]   Ibid., p. 19.

communicating with other men. The consequence of this was that, for the first time in the history of mankind, a High Culture becomes the pervasive culture of an entire society, instead of being a minority accomplishment and privilege. The expression 'High Culture' is of course here used in a sociological and not in an evaluative sense: it means a standardized culture transmitted by professional educators in accordance with fairly rigid, coded norms, and with the help of literacy, as opposed to a 'Low Culture' transmitted without formal education in the course of other and generally unspecialized activities of life.

The third stage would be that of Nationalism Triumphant and Self-defeating after 1918. As Carr observes, the first successes of nationalism, the unifactory nationalisms of the Italians and the Germans, diminished the number of political units in Europe, whilst the later period dramatically increased it. But the new units set up in 1918 had all the defects of those alleged prison-houses of nations (or should one say, nurseries of nations and nationalisms) which they replaced, plus some additional ones of their own. They were just as minority-haunted, but they were smaller, unhallowed by age and often without experienced leaders, while the minorities whose irredentism they had to face included members of previously dominant cultural groups, unused to subordination and well-placed to resist it. The weakness of this system soon became manifest: in the age of Hitler and Stalin, it collapsed with very little resistance, and no effective resistance (with the remarkable exception of Finland).

There then comes the fourth stage, which I like to characterize by the expression used by the Nazis for some of their wartime operations: *Nacht und Nebel*. Under cover of night and fog, of wartime secrecy, and also under the protection of the immediate post-war indignation which allowed severe retaliatory measures, practices were possible from which otherwise men shrink. The nationalist principle of social organization requires, in effect, the marriage of polity and culture: a state becomes a protector of a culture, and one gains citizenship in virtue of participating in a culture (and also, satisfying its prescribed self-image), rather than in virtue of lineage, residence, property or anything else. The nationalist principle is extremely difficult to satisfy in conditions of great cultural ('ethnic') diversity, where villages of quite different languages are juxtaposed, and where culture and language are often functions not of position on the geographical map, but of social role and stratum. The linguistic–cultural *Gleichschaltung* of populations had previously been achieved, in the main, by the relatively humane method of assimilation, whether voluntary (sometimes enthusiastic) or so to speak prodded. Now, under the cover of *Nacht und Nebel*, obscured by secrecy or licensed by a temporary moral *sursis*, other methods could be and were employed: mass murder and forcible transplantation of populations. Under Hitler's and Stalin's auspices, the ethno-political map of Central and Eastern Europe was much, though not completely, simplified.

Why did nationalism become so particularly ferocious in this period? A century of thwarting the nationalist aspiration, followed in 1918 by a political Paul Jones in which privilege and humiliation were redistributed at random, may be one factor. The visible correlation of prosperity and cultural group, characteristic of early industrialism, is another: the difference between the mildly affluent and the indigent produces more bitterness than the later industrial difference between the affluent and the very affluent. There was also the survival of what might be called peasant–military thinking: the supposition that wealth and standing depend on control of land. (It was only the economic success of the vanquished after 1945, and the economic decline of some victors, which finally dissolved this association of ideas.) And there was also an ideological element. At the start, nationalist ideology was benign, almost timid: it preached the value of and respect for idiosyncratic peasant cultures against the centralizing tendencies of Versailles court models or British commercialism and empiricism in particular, and against the universalism of the Enlightenment in general. Though deeply rooted in the new *Gesellschaft*, it preached the ideals of the closed *Gemeinschaft*. But by the latter part of the century, Herder was joined by Darwin and by the Nietzschean twist to biologism. The community to be re-drawn, revived or re-awakened was seen as not merely cultural but also genetic. This was joined to the view that ruthlessness is both the precondition of excellence and the accompaniment of true human fulfilment, as opposed to the anaemic cosmopolitan values of the Enlightenment, which do not truly correspond to the needs of the human psyche. Somewhere in this mix of factors one can find the explanation of the really extreme excesses of nationalism in this period. Carr, interestingly, considers the tendency towards totalitarianism to be inherent in nationalism.

There is a fifth stage, half speculation, half wish-fulfilment, and perhaps endowed with a small dose of factual support as well. Late industrialism in some places and in some measure leads to a diminution of the intensity of ethnic sentiments and hostilities. There is an element of truth in the Convergence Thesis: advanced industrial societies, at least when they started from a reasonably similar starting point, come to resemble each other. Differences between languages become phonetic rather than semantic: similar concepts are clothed in diverse sounds, but the concepts do come closer to each other. Generalized affluence diminishes intensity of hatreds, and gives everyone that much more to lose in case of violent conflict. These arguments are not overwhelmingly powerful and certainly cannot be treated as some guarantee of a harmonious future, but they provide a small measure of licence for hope.

These five stages represent a plausible account of the transition from a non-nationalist society with a static technology and stable hierarchy, in which culture is used mainly to indicate the status of individuals and groups in the overall structure rather than marking the bounds of a pervasive polity, to a nationalist order characterized by anonymous mobile masses who share a literate culture transmitted by an educational system and who are protected by a state identified with that culture. If these are indeed the five as it were normal, natural stages of the transition, certain important observations must be made concerning the actual manifestations of these stages in Europe. It was all, in a systematic way, rather different in different places.

Time Zones of Europe

From the viewpoint of the ethnic impact on politics, Europe has as it were four time zones, very distinct from each other. Going from West to East, there is first of all the Atlantic sea-coast. Here, from early modern times or earlier, there were strong dynastic states. The political units based on Lisbon, Madrid, Paris and London, correlated roughly, though of course far from completely, with cultural–linguistic regions. Come the age of nationalism, and the requirement of cultural homogeneity within any one polity, relatively very little re-drawing of frontiers was required: the emergence of the Republic of Ireland is the only clear case of it. (It is not clear whether the separation of Belgium from Holland and of Norway from Sweden should count as specimens of modern nationalism.) The consequence of this is that in this zone there is little of what might be called ethnographic nationalism: the study, codification and idealization of peasant cultures in the interest of forging a new national culture. On the contrary, in terms of the title of Eugene Weber's book, the problem was rather that of turning *peasants into Frenchmen*, rather than inventing a new culture on the basis of peasant idiosyncrasy.[4] Ernest Renan, who understood the logic of the situation, insisted that nationality was based on forgetting, not on remembrance (or, he might have said, on invented memories). In his celebrated essay on the subject, he insisted that the French could not consistently invoke both a voluntaristic and an ethnographic definition of their identity and boundaries.[5]

Europe's second time zone is somewhat different. It corresponds, in the main, to the territory of the erstwhile Holy Roman Empire. The main characteristic of this zone is that the two cultures which make up the majority of its inhabitants have been extremely well endowed, for a long time, with a well-defined High Culture, sustained by an extensive literate class. Ever since

[4]   Eugene Weber, *Peasants into Frenchmen* (London, 1979).
[5]   Ernest Renan, 'Qu'est-ce qu'une nation?', in *Ernest Renan et l'Allemagne*, textes recueillis et commentés par Émile Bure (New York, 1945).

the Renaissance and the Reformation, if not longer, a well-articulated Italian and German High Culture existed. Perhaps those who self-consciously created a German literature in the late eighteenth century had to standardize spelling a bit, but nevertheless they were fortifying, not creating a national culture. In literacy, sophistication and self-awareness, the Germans were not significantly (if at all) inferior to the French, and the same holds of the relationship of the Italians to the Austrians. So all that nationalism needed to do here was to endow an existing High Culture, well suited to define a modern nation, with its political roof. A number of battles and much diplomatic activity were required, but no other and more extreme measures were called for.

Things were different in the third zone further East. It was here that all the five stages, postulated earlier, played themselves out to the full. Here, in the main, there were neither well-defined and well-sustained High Cultures, nor any political shells to cover and protect them. There were only the old non-national empires and the patchwork of folk cultures and cultural diversities separating social strata as well as distinguishing adjoining territories. In the marriage between culture and polity which is required by nationalism, *both* partners had to be brought into existence before they could be joined unto each other. This made the task of the nationalists correspondingly more arduous and hence, often, its execution more brutal. Here, there was hardly any need of the exacerbation of feelings and the legitimation of violence provided by Darwin as interpreted by Nietzsche.

The fourth zone is further East still. It shared the 'normal' trajectory with Zone Three until 1918 or the early 1920s. But then, whilst two of the three defeated empires remained on the dustheap of history (all three were defeated by 1918 even though they had not been on the same side in the War), one of them was dramatically revived, under entirely new management and in the name of a new, inspiring, passionately held and ruthlessly imposed ideology. To complicate matters a little, as a result of the victorious advance of the Red Army in 1945, a good part of Zone Three was incorporated in Zone Four, and shared its fate till the dismemberment of the revived and expanded empire in and after 1989.

The new ideocracy was as least as successful in keeping nationalism at bay as the mixture of political *ancien régime* and economic *laissez-faire* had been in nineteenth-century Europe. But this was not merely an absolutist ideocracy, but an absolutist socialism which did not tolerate economic, political or ideological pluralism. In other words, it effectively destroyed civil society. It did not, however, fail to produce those social conditions which lead to nationalism, i.e. to the identification of men with a High Culture which defines a large, mobile, anonymous mass of people, who however visualize that abstract society in the imagery of a concrete community. Result: when the system dismantles itself, nationalism emerges with all its vigour, but with few of its rivals. Zone Four having been artificially frozen at the end of the second stage, it remains to be seen whether it slots itself into the 'normal' sequence at stage three, four or five – i.e. whether irredentist nationalism, or massacres and population movements, or a diminution of ethnic conflict in the interest of a federal–cantonal cooperation, will predominate. Each of these elements is present, and no one knows which one will prevail.

Assessment of Carr's Analysis

Carr could not be expected to foresee that the peacemakers of 1945 would be rewarded, like those of 1815 (but very much unlike those of 1918, whose fate was so much in the forefront of Carr's mind), with the windfall of a politically mollifying prosperity, though on a very much larger, more dramatic scale, and above all, more quickly. Nor could he foresee – virtually no one did – that the relative ineffectiveness of the rival economic system practised and imposed in Eastern Europe, would be so dreadful, and recognized as such by the very leaders of the polity, that they should themselves proceed to dismantle it, despite the cost to themselves (which they perhaps did not fully appreciate when they initiated the process). So he could not foresee that, around 1990, we should once again see that proliferation of political units which he noted and deplored in connection with the settlement of 1918.

Although Carr was master of all the relevant facts, he did not formally distinguish between the four time zones or spell out in so many words that their respective situations had a different kind of logic. If you take the Westernmost time zone as your basic model (possibly adding Prussia, which after all did not disappear in the nineteenth century, but eventually expanded to become Germany), it is of course tempting to see the age of nationalism as a kind of continuation of the emergence of sovereign states, differing only in the fact that the nature of the sovereign within each state moves from a person to a culturally homogeneous population. It also becomes a kind of curiosity, rather than a central fact, that the impact of nationalism in the second zone leads to a diminution in the number of political units, whereas in the third it leads to their multiplication. But what really matters is: who exactly is the hero, the subject of the story? For Carr, it is the European state, or perhaps the European state system. Nationalism, and the social factors helping to engender it, enter above all as catalysts in the development of the state. The alternative way of writing the story is to look at society, or nationalism itself, as the subject, and then consider the impact which a pervasive and internally coherent social transformation has on states. The two formulations can be, without undue difficulty, translated into each other: in other words, Carr already knew it all. He puts it as follows:

> Intellectually the transition from Frederick to Napoleon was paralleled by the transition from Gibbon to Burke, or from Goethe and Lessing to Herder and Schiller; the cosmopolitanism of the Enlightenment was replaced by the nationalism of the romantic movement . . . The nation in its new and popular connotation had come to stay. International relations were henceforth to be governed not by the personal interests, ambitions and emotions of the monarch, but by the collective interests, ambitions and emotions of the nation.[6]

[6]   Carr, *Nationalism*, p. 8.

It is all there, but the focus of his interest, in the end, is 'international relations'. The focus ought to be, it seems to me, society itself: just why had it changed internally, so that the subject of history should no longer be either monarchs, estates or other structurally identified individuals or groups, but instead, internally fairly undifferentiated, mobile, anonymous populations, united by a shared literate culture, one requiring and demanding a political protector identified with it, and sharply separated by conspicuous and politically underwritten boundaries from other such groups? *This* is the change which really matters, and it deserves to be the central, rather than a minor character in the drama.

Specific predictions on points of relative detail do not really matter too much. What is perhaps of greater interest is the standing of his analysis as a whole. Here, the assessment of his vision will obviously depend on who is speaking, on the position from which he is being evaluated. Those of us who see nationalism as the playing out of forces inherent in the switch from agrarian to industrial society will be strongly inclined to admire the lucidity and accuracy of his vision. He saw the way in which nationalism meshed in with the other great changes, and he certainly saw more connections than, for instance, I could see, no doubt because of his greater knowledge and because he was a historian rather than a sociological model-builder. But he saw it all from a slightly strange angle: the big changes come in as so to speak extraneous characters, making their impact on what interested him most – the international order. The fact that these changes were inherently related to each other, that they were all parts of one big process, and that in the end they had a similar impact on the structurally quite distinct 'time zones' of Europe, all that – though no doubt he would have recognized it – is not underscored in his study of nationalism. In a sense he asks what nationalism does to a pre-existent polity or system of polities rather than why nationalism is now at the centre of the social stage. But although he looks at it all from a different angle, his unjustly neglected essay remains of great contemporary interest.

3

From Kinship to Ethnicity

A marked feature of the nineteenth and twentieth centuries is the political salience of ethnic feeling. Western liberal social thought and Marxism are united in this at least – they have committed the same error: both have under-estimated the political vigour of nationalism. Now, after nearly two centuries of experience of political nationalism, the time is perhaps ripe to understand why we were both jointly mistaken. We must attempt to correct the error which unites us.*

The error was very natural. With the wisdom of hindsight, we now know that it was indeed an error. But we should not allow ourselves any feelings of superiority over our predecessors. The premisses from which they reasoned were valid ones. Their view was based on a perceptive and, as far as it went, perfectly sound account of the impact of industrialism on human society. If the conclusions drawn from those perfectly valid insights did not, in the end, completely tally with all the realities of the situation – if, in other words, nationalist political sentiment increased rather than diminished in this period – then this must be due to the operation of factors which were not easy to discern in advance. Perhaps they are still not properly understood. In attempting to

* This essay was originally presented to a Soviet audience prior to the dis-establishment of Marxism.

comprehend what has happened, we are correcting our own errors as well as those of our predecessors.

The premisses which, very plausibly and convincingly, led to an anticipation of the decline of nationalism, can be summed up as follows.

Complex pre-industrial civilizations (in Marxist terms: feudal, slave and Asiatic societies) are endowed with a very complicated division of labour, which is accompanied and in a way confirmed or even sanctified, by great cultural diversity. Linguistic, sartorial, gastronomic, ritual, doctrinal variety abounds. People express and recognize their identity in these idiosyncratic features of their social station. A man *is* not merely (as the German pun insists) what he *eats*, he is also what he speaks, wears, dances, whom he may eat with, speak with, marry, etc., and so forth. Frequently, he *is* what he does *not* eat.

'Ethnicity' or 'nationality' is simply the name for the condition which prevails when many of these boundaries converge and overlap, so that the boundaries of conversation, easy commensality, shared pastimes, etc., are the same, and when the community of people delimited by these boundaries is endowed with an ethnonym, and is suffused with powerful feelings. Ethnicity becomes 'political', it gives rise to a 'nationalism', when the 'ethnic' group defined by these overlapping cultural boundaries is not merely acutely conscious of its own existence, but also imbued with the conviction that the ethnic boundary ought also to be a political one. The requirement is that the boundaries of ethnicity should also be the boundaries of the political unit, and, above all, that the rulers within that unit should be of the same ethnicity as the ruled. Foreigners, at any rate in large numbers, are unwelcome in the political unit, and quite particularly unwelcome as *rulers*.

It is possible to put forward the following hypothesis about pre-industrial civilizations: they are very richly endowed with cultural and hence (potentially or actually) ethnic differences, but nevertheless, *political* nationalisms are rare. The requirement that the political unit be homogeneous culturally, and conversely, that each culture should possess its own (and preferably no more than one) political unit, which is to be co-extensive with that culture, is seldom affirmed, and even more seldom implemented. On the contrary in these conditions, the cultural (and hence 'ethnic') differentiation of diverse layers of the population, including the rulers, is highly functional, seldom resented and often warmly approved. The cultural differentiation constitutes a kind of externalization or visible manifestation of diverse stable ranks and roles, and thereby diminishes ambiguity and friction. The ranking and role systems are confirmed and strengthened by cultural nuance. Differences in speech, dress, manner, appearance, are indicators of the rights and duties of their possessors.

Industrialism destroys the intricate social differentiation which found its external expression and confirmation, sometimes quite literally its sacrament, in cultural diversity. Marx and Engels focused on the fact that under capitalism labour becomes a *commodity*, to be bought and sold in the light of demand and supply, without any reference to the identity and social location of the labourer. The total detachment of labour from the social identity of the person performing it was a significant element in the Marxist notion of 'alienation'.

Later capitalism does not in all respects resemble Engels' Manchester, and contemporary 'skilled labour' has lost some of that undifferentiated, levelled-out quality: modern capitalists wishing to purchase raw, undifferentiated muscle power, need to import it from the Third World (West Indians in Britain, Algerians in France, Turks in Germany). Nevertheless, modern skilled labour retains that structure-eroding quality which marked its predecessor. The modern industrial worker no longer arrives from a village, driven out by enclosures or by collectivization: he comes from a housing estate in an industrial town, and he is prepared for his work by a universal schooling system. His important skills are *generic*; they include literacy, the capacity to read, interpret and observe written instructions, to operate a sophisticated machine which will soon break down if the instructions are ignored. The worker's skills are semantic: he must have the training which will enable him to translate the precepts of a manual of instruction into the ability to press the right button, or to adjust the control at the right time. These skills can be transferred from one machine to another, one control system to another, and they are recorded and transmitted in terms of a code which is general, and tied, not to a guild, but to a national educational system. They enable the modern worker to switch from one job to another given a little rapid retraining.

So the modern skilled worker, like his less fortunate ancestor, the unskilled early industrial worker, is not tied to any particular social niche. The system of such niches thereby becomes weakened, or altogether obliterated. The typical modern industrial worker is no longer as mobile geographically as was his ancestor, or as is his contemporary the *Gastarbeiter*, and the commodity labour, which he sells, is no longer so undifferentiated as to be sold, as it were, by weight or time: nevertheless, his links to the means of production are not such as to engender a complicated system of status, such as prevailed in traditional society, and which sustained its rich, nuanced cultural variety.

This then is the crucial, insightful and exceedingly persuasive premise, shared alike by classical Marxism, classical liberal theory, and also by a great deal of modern sociological theory: the work conditions of industrial society are such as to erode those very structures which sustain cultural difference. Cultural differences will be flattened out by the bulldozer of industrial production. Ethnicity consists of overlapping, mutually reinforcing cultural differences. So ethnicity will go down the drain, alongside these cultural differences which make it visible, and are of its essence.

So the syllogism which irresistibly imposes itself on us is the following:

1   Industrial social organization erodes social structures.
2   Cultural differences arise from, and are sustained by, structural differentiation.
3   'Ethnicity' consists of superimposed, mutually reinforcing cultural differences. These lead their possessors to identify with their culture, and to be opposed to carriers of other, rival cultures.

Conclusion

4　Eroded structure means loss of cultural differentiation. This in turn means loss of ethnic identification. So ethnicity must lose its political significance.

In other words, the withering away of nationalism is inevitable. In even simpler terms: the more industrialism, the less nationalism.

It seems to me that there simply cannot be any reasonable doubt concerning the truth of the three crucial premises 1, 2 and 3. Equally, it would be hard to deny that the conclusion, 4, does follow from these premises.

No wonder that so many thinkers of great distinction have accepted, or tacitly assumed, the validity of the conclusion. Moreover, the conclusion continues to contain important elements of truth.

Nevertheless – and this is our central problem – proposition 4 is *not* an accurate reflection of the political realities of the nineteenth and twentieth centuries. Nationalism has in fact *grown* in importance; not evenly, not without encountering obstacles and occasional defeats, but, all in all, with ever increasing vigour. As a principle of political organization, the idea that political boundaries must be congruent with ethnic ones, that rulers must not be ethnically distinguishable from the ruled, now has a salience and authority which it has never possessed in the previous history of mankind. This is a fact which we must face. It presents us with a problem which is as intriguing theoretically as it is important practically. Yet the argument which had led so many thinkers of distinction to the opposite conclusion was plausible, persuasive, logical and based on perfectly valid premises. What went wrong? What did we leave out? Herewith is an attempt to answer this question.

Pre-industrial agrarian society is one in which the overwhelming majority of the population lives the life of agricultural producers, and spends its life within the bounds of small self-contained communities ('the idiocy of rural life' – Karl Marx).

Russia, for instance, was still such a country at the beginning of this century. The cultural consequences of such a situation are fairly obvious. Village communities possess neither the means nor the need for literacy, or for the art of abstract communication. People who spend their lives in stable social contexts, facing repetitive and standard situations, involved with the same people, communicate with each other by intonation, posture, facial expression: language for them is a stylized art form, like their folk dances, and it is not at all a machine for the production of infinitely varied, context-free messages (this being, in effect, the Chomskian definition of language). Only the higher strata of an agrarian society (and by no means all of its members) are able to use language in an abstract, context-free manner, and live a life within which such a capacity possesses a function, and is socially acceptable. For a peasant, to speak in such a manner would constitute a remarkable piece of insolence, and might well earn him a whipping. Who does he think he is?

In general, within such a society, there is a marked discontinuity between High Culture and Low Culture, or between High Tradition and Little Tradition. The political relationship between the two layers varies from case to case. High Culture is so to speak normative; it considers itself to be the model of human comportment, and it spurns Low Culture as a miserable distortion or aberration. It may treat Low Culture with indifference as well as contempt, or alternatively it may feel that, in a perfect world, Low Culture should be transformed in its own image.

Within Islam, for instance, the scholars, the *ulama*, are the guardians of moral, political and theological legitimacy, and consider folk deviations from their Koranic standards to constitute a scandal. From time to time they attempt (never successfully, until the coming of the modern world) to convert the tribal, rustic and urban low-class world to their own standards. Islam is imbued with an internal as well as external missionary zeal, and constitutes a kind of Permanent Reformation. The real social circumstances have never allowed this internal jihad to be permanently successful, at any rate until the coming of modern administrative, military and productive technology: these have now enabled the ever-present drive to be, at long last, successful. This is the secret underlying the otherwise puzzling political vigour of contemporary Muslim fundamentalism. In Hinduism, by contrast, the upper brahmanical layer attempts, virtually by definition, to monopolize human perfection for itself, excluding others, so to speak, from full and unpolluted humanity. It is the lower castes who attempt to steal the sacred fire, by emulating their betters (a process described as 'Sanskritization' by the Indian sociologist Srinivas). In North-western Europe, Protestantism, by its stress on literacy, symmetry of access to the deity and its message, in other words, the universalization of the clerisy, was successful to a remarkable extent in diminishing the chasm between High and Low Culture, thereby helping to prepare the ground both for capitalism and for the early emergence of political nationalism.

So the details vary a great deal from one agrarian–literate civilization to another. What concerns us here is the shared general pattern: a discontinuity between a high, literate, education-transmitted, spiritually formulated culture, and a low, oral culture, transmitted from generation to generation without much or any assistance from full-time cultural specialists or script-recorded prescriptive models. This deep division is the standard and pervasive cultural condition of mankind in the agrarian age. It is not rooted, as the proselytizing representatives of the high and normative cultural order often think, in human weakness, or in the depravity of the lower orders. It is based on the real material conditions prevalent in that age, which limit the possibilities of cultural life. Peasants cannot be either scholars or scholastics; they dance, sing and live their culture, but they cannot read or write it. It is not weakness of the flesh, but the demands of the system of social production, reproduction and self-maintenance, which dictate that most men fail to fulfil the dominant ideals of their own culture.

The work situation of modern industrial man is entirely different. Only a small percentage of the working population tills the land. Even those who do so, employ tools which resemble those of industrial work. A good tractor driver is a man who has mastered the semantics of the control system of a moderately complex machine, and who knows how to use it and maintain it in accordance with the prescriptions of a printed manual.

For the great majority of the population, 'work' means the

manipulation of meanings and of people, not of things. Work is the interpretation, selection and transmission of messages, not the direct transformation of nature by brawn. The increasing sophistication of industrial production means that the labourer is not a man wielding a pick and a shovel, but a skilled master of the control system of a machine tool. The office worker, when not brewing tea, receives and emits messages by phone, type-writer, telex and so forth.

The modern industrial world is one in which, for the first time in human history, high or literate or education-transmitted culture is no longer a minority privilege and monopoly. It has become the pervasive possession of the overwhelming majority of the population. The citizen of modern society owes his employ-ability, his cultural participation, his moral citizenship, his capacity to deal with the all-pervasive bureaucracy, not to skills acquired at his mother's knee or on the village green, or even from his master in the course of a workshop apprenticeship: he owes it to skills which can only be acquired by passing through a pervasive, all-embracing, educational system, operating in a standardized linguistic medium, transmitting information contained in manuals rather than in cultural context, and depending on the well-diffused ability to receive, understand, react to and transmit messages to anonymous interlocutors, independently of context. Without the possession of such skills, a member of modern society is rendered helpless, and finds himself demoted to the lowest layers of society. The persons with whom modern man interacts are not drawn from a restricted group of fellow-villagers, whom he knows intimately; they are drawn from an enormously large number of fellow members of an anonymous mass society, communicating by means of a literate, abstract High Culture. Consequence: by far the most important investment or possession of modern man is his access to that shared literate High Culture, which is the medium of a viable industrial system. Because he values this investment, he becomes a nationalist.

Entry into or access to such a system depends on two factors: (1) mastery of the required skills, as indicated, and (2) possession of personal attributes compatible with the self-image of the culture in question. The nature and implications of the first condition have already been considered. The second one is also important.

If mastery of the skills required to operate and fit in with the semantically sophisticated tools of the late industrial society were *all* that were needed to be a full member of such a society, one would expect a kind of late-industrial internationalism to arise, a brotherhood of all those who had passed the rites of initiation into the mysteries of modern technology. This was anticipated by both liberals and Marxists, but it has not happened. There are indeed *some* hints of such a development; there is said to be a kind of cosmopolitan brotherhood of the personnel of the large multinational corporations, and something similar amongst the members of specialized professions (oil-men, mathematicians, even an informal International of military men), cutting across 'national' boundaries. But industrial cosmopolitanism, so to speak, is incomparably less conspicuous in our age than the emphatic, sometimes violent affirmation of national delimitation and sentiment. What is the explanation?

1 The High Culture which, for the first time in human history, pervades entire societies, is not simply made up of formal skills such as literacy as such, the capacity to operate computers, read manuals, observe technical instructions. It has to be articulated in some definite language, such as Russian or English or Arabic, and it must also contain rules for comportment in life; in other words, it must contain a 'culture' in the sense in which ethnographers use the term. Nineteenth- and twentieth-century man does not merely industrialize, he industrializes *as* a German or Russian or Japanese. Those excluded from the new community are excluded not merely in virtue of having failed to acquire the necessary skills, but also in virtue of having acquired them in the 'wrong' idiom. Modern industrial High Culture is not colourless; it has an 'ethnic' colouring, which is of its essence. The cultural norm incorporates expectations, requirements and prescriptions, which impose obligations on its members. An Englishman is expected not merely to speak the language of Shakespeare, but also to be white – which imposes problems for men who by birth,

language and culture are English, but who by pigmentation fail to conform to the expected stereotype. Poles or Croats are meant to be Catholic, Persians are meant to be Shi'ite, Frenchmen are meant to be, not Catholic perhaps, but at any rate *not* Muslim.

2 Industrialism, the comir. of the modern productive equipment, notoriously does not hit all mankind simultaneously. On the contrary it arrives unevenly, creating enormous disparities of development, great inequalities in wealth and in economic and political power. Enormous and painful frictions and conflict develop at the boundaries between more and less developed populations. Strong incentives exist for the setting up of frontiers and exclusion, *both* among the more *and* among the less developed groups. The more highly developed regions do admittedly import cheap labour from the less developed ones, but generally dislike sharing full citizenship, and the high level of social infrastructure, with the recently arrived and culturally distinguishable pariahs. Penury and discrimination drive the latter, or some of them, into a criminal underworld, which further reinforces prejudice against them. The resulting situation strengthens nationalist sentiments amongst *both* populations.

There is a further important factor. Under conditions of capitalism or the free market, backward regions cannot easily develop, being thwarted by the effective competition of more advanced areas. They need to insulate themselves. If already possessed of an effective centralized leadership, such development will be pursued by means of economic or political and cultural insulation and protection, in the interest of securing the desired political and military strength for the elite in question and the unit over which it presides. If the backward area in question has been incorporated in a colonial or a territorially continuous empire, the local elites perceive the advantage of setting up a separate unit, within which they will possess the monopoly of access to political and other positions, instead of needing to compete in a larger unit, with rivals favoured by a better-established educational tradition. On all these assumptions, the setting up of a separate political unit linked to its own standardized educational system and hence its own cultural symbolism and image, is attractive and will be attempted whenever circumstances are favourable.

This, then, is our overall scenario of the transition from pre-industrial non-nationalistic societies to industrial nationalist ones: in the former, a great wealth of cultural differentiations, often cutting across each other, does not on the whole give rise to political turbulence. On the contrary, it tends to underwrite and support existing social and political structures. By contrast, the standardization of productive activities under conditions of industrial production produces a set of internally homogeneous, externally differentiated political units, which are both cultural and political. The political unit (the state) is a protector of a culture, the culture is the symbolism and legitimation of the state. The English monarch is officially defined as the protector of a *faith*, but in reality the modern English state protects a *culture*, not a doctrine.

The number of these units on our globe is far smaller than that of the *earlier* cultural differences. Their borders now reflect, in part, the limits of some of the major pre-industrial cultures, and in part, the points of friction which became septic through uneven development during the drive towards industrialization. Minor cultural units and nuances tend to disappear; but major ones become very significant politically. This is the central story.

This theory can perhaps claim to be a specimen of historical materialism, in as far as it links the phenomenon with which it is concerned – nationalism – to the basic mode of production of the age in which nationalism becomes prominent. It differs from classical historical materialism at two points: it fully recognizes the increasing vigour of political nationalism – that after all is the problem with which our argument begins – and secondly, it focuses, not on the ownership or control of capital, but on the nature and implications of the types of skills and activities which are involved in modern forms of production.

The theory does explain why nationalism, relatively inconspicuous in the past, is so very salient in our age. It explains why the social prominence of cultural nuance has *diminished* whilst, at the same time, the political significance of the few surviving cultural boundaries has greatly *increased*. On the other hand, it cannot explain all aspects of our contemporary situation. It does not explain why, for instance, German nationalism should have become quite so virulent during the Nazi period. Or again, it fails to explain the firm commitment of anglophone Canadians to the existing Canadian political unit, notwithstanding the fact that anglophone Canadians at any rate have not the slightest difficulty in operating within the polity of the USA.

What can this theory offer to those grappling with nationalist turbulence in the real world?

1 A sense of the need for sober realism. The appeal of cultural ('ethnic') identity is not a delusion, excogitated by muddled romantics, disseminated by irresponsible extremists, and used by egotistical privileged classes to befuddle the masses, and to hide their true interests from them. Its appeal is rooted in the real conditions of modern life, and cannot be conjured away, either by sheer good will and the preaching of a spirit of universal brotherhood, or by the incarceration of the extremists. We have to understand those roots, and live with their fruits, whether we like them or not.

Adjustment to the new realities cannot always be painless, alas. The pre-industrial world has bequeathed to us a complex patchwork of cultural differences – and stratifications – and many ethnicity-blind boundaries. Modern conditions imply an egalitarianism (whose roots are similar to those of nationalism) which, unlike the old condition, is deeply averse to the linkage of privilege – or under-privilege – to ethnic differentiation. It tolerates a fair measure of privilege, but not its brazen cultural or ethnic externalization. It is also rather allergic to the non-congruence of political and ethnic boundaries. The correction of all these ethnicity-defying survivals from an earlier age cannot always be agreeable and pleasant. We are fortunate when it can be achieved by mere assimilation and frontier rectification, without the use of the more brutal methods deployed in the course of this century (genocide, forcible transplantation).

2   There are some grounds for partial optimism. The diffusion of economic prosperity can diminish the intensity of ethnic feelings. When two populations, previously in ethnic conflict, both possess favourable and reasonably equal economic prospects, then the acute friction which is engendered by inequality of economic development, and made visible and offensive by cultural 'ethnic' differences, gradually disappears. It is possible to think of examples of this, and hope that they will become more general.

But to sum up: pre-industrial complex societies were endowed with elaborate and fairly stable structures, systems of roles. Kinship provided these roles not merely with much of their terminology, but genuinely played a major part in the mechanism of allocating individuals to their positions. As a consequence of the nature of work in industrial society, and of the occupational mobility which is inherent in the pursuit of economic growth (which in turn constitutes the main principle of political legitimation), kinship loses a great deal of this kind of importance. The terminology and ideology, and in good measure, the actual mechanism of allocation to social position is bureaucratic and meritocratic. But the nature of work also requires men to be identified with a High (i.e. literate, school-transmitted) Culture. The internalization of such a culture, and the conformity with its expectation which ensures his admission into it, constitute a person's identity, to a far greater extent than they did in the past. In a sense, ethnicity has replaced kinship as the principal method of identity-conferment.

Recent Soviet work in this field includes: Yu. V. Bromley, *Natsional'nve Protsessy v SSSR*, Nauka, 1988; also 'Natsionalnye Problemy v Uslovyakh Perestroiki', *Voprosy Istorii*, N.1, 1989; G. Guseinov, 'Ideologia Obschchevo Doma', *Vek XX i Mir*, N.1, 1989; V. I. Kozlov, 'Natsionalnyi Vopros. Kontseptsii i Alternativi', *Sovietska Etnografia*, N.1, 1989; I. Krupnik, 'Mnogonatsionalnoe Obshehestvo', *Sovietskaia Ethnografia*, N.1, 1989; V. Tishkov, 'Narody i Gosudarstvo', *Kommunist*, 1 (1335), Yanvar, 1989; V. Tishkov, 'Vse my luidi. Razmyshlenie o etnicheskom samosoznaniu', *Znanie Sila*, 4/1989.

4

The Betrayal of the Universal

The most celebrated sermon concerning the responsibility of intellectuals is perhaps Julien Benda's *La Trahison des clercs*.[1] Its argument is articulated against an uncritically assumed background of Platonic metaphysics and universalistic ethics. A realm of values binding all men alike is simply presupposed. The 'clercs' are rebuked for abandoning these, and for whoring after local and particularistic idols.

[1] Julien Benda (1867–1956) wrote this work between 1924 and 1927 and published it in Paris in 1928. It is the response of this celebrated essayist and political commentator to what he perceived to be a severe crisis in European culture. The book takes the form of an essay in historical sociology. Benda asserts that up to the late nineteenth century, there had been two broad classes of men, the 'clercs' and the 'lay people': the latter were involved in the practical running of society and the application of thought and science to it; the former were those who were not active in the pursuit or support of practical aims, but who stood aside from their society and argued for non-immediate, non-material, disinterested values. The 'treason' of the 'clercs' of the late nineteenth century was manifested in their involvement in practical political life, and in their acceptance that intellectual activity could be harnessed to political, nationalistic and racial ends. This gave to the discreditable ideologies of 'lay people' the respectability of a systematic and coherent doctrine, lending them enhanced credibility and authority. Benda predicted that separation of function of 'clerc' and 'lay person' was crucial to the survival of European civilization, and his diagnosis of the breakdown of this division of roles prophetically pointed to the holocaust and other tragic events of the Second World War. (Ed.)

As an account of much that had come to pass in the nine-teenth and twentieth centuries, no doubt this was accurate enough. The monotheism which had dominated Europe for so long was both exclusive and universalist in its claims: one truth and one only was there for all and binding on all. Those who deviated from it were wrong, and those who deviated from it out of a loyalty to local and specific idols were traitors to truth. The theologians who codified the theory implicit in this faith did so roughly speaking in Platonistic terms, even if they happened to be nominalists. The truth was unique, incorruptible and authori-tative because it was transcendent.

The task of literate intellectuals was to preserve, communicate and impose the truth which was in their keeping, and to which they had privileged access. The access was made possible both through Scripture and a Special Institution linked to the point of Revelation, and with the Reformation, these two methods of validation came into open conflict. But they were at one in pre-supposing and proclaiming a single and universally binding truth. The position differed from Platonism proper, of course, in per-sonalizing the Transcendent, and in possessing a narrative ac-count concerning the manner in which the Transcendent communicated with the world and by stressing the role which the Transcendent played, not merely in providing a yardstick, but also in actually creating the world. But these details apart, the background picture, the contrast of a towering Normative Other and a subordinated Here-Now, was genuinely Platonic. It engen-dered a tension between Transcendent and Authoritative Other and the earthly Here-Now, and turned the scholar–cleric into an emissary and agent of the Other on earth.[2]

The Reformation, paradoxically, re-affirmed the universality of the message, by stressing symmetrical and equal access to it: yet it also contained the seeds of fragmentation. Its stress on the vernacular and on literacy jointly paved the ground for the em-ployment, and eventually even the authority, of local cultures, in

---

[2]   See S. N. Eisenstadt (ed.), *Axial Age Civilisations*, Albany: State University of New York, 1986.

other words for nationalism. Its stress on autonomy of interpretation prepared the ground for a relativism as opposed to a universalism.

The Enlightenment challenged the Revealed truth and its institutional guardians, but once again did not really challenge the metaphysical idiom in which the faith had been codified. The preachers of Enlightenment took that for granted, and merely elaborated a counter-doctrine roughly in the same terms, and endowed with the same universalist pretensions.[3] If there was a conflict between their characteristically naturalistic views, and the universalism rooted in a now obsolete transcendentalism, they did not properly face it, or supposed they could find a logical way of making them compatible. (Cognitive functions *within* nature could be expected to vary, like all natural organs; so why should there be a single truth for all organisms, biological or social? Yet a unique truth *about* nature was assumed to obtain!) They remained guardians of a universal and unique truth, even if the content of the message had been transformed. In fact, they saw themselves primarily as the messengers of a secular but unique Revelation, and made themselves into its very vocal propagandists.

It was the Romantic reaction to the Enlightenment, on the surface an attempt to return to some earlier, pre-Enlightenment forms of life, which in reality repudiated something that both the Enlightenment and the theological age had *shared*: the universalist assumption. Emotion and cultural specificity, joined to a denial of the primacy of a universal, cosmopolitan Reason, became fashionable. This was the beginning of the treason of the clercs, so vociferously denounced by Benda.

My main point is going to be simple: *La Trahison des clercs* was itself a case of 'la trahison des clercs'.

Let me illustrate this by means of an example. Assume, for instance, the truth of a naturalistic theory of knowledge. This is, after all, by no means an absurd assumption. It might even be considered a necessary truth: rational inquiry presupposes that

---

[3] See C. L. Becker, *The Heavenly City of the Eighteenth Century Philosophers*, New Haven: Yale University Press, 1952.

the world constitutes a single, orderly system, in other words a 'nature'. Hence creatures within nature cannot claim exemption from its laws: what each of them considers 'knowledge' cannot possibly be a relationship between it and something eternal and transcending the system. It can only be an inevitably selective, functional set of adjustments between its own *specific* nature and its variable environment. The adjustment can only be validated by its functional effectiveness, not by conformity to some universal Norm. It is inescapably tied to transient circumstances. The relativity of the functional adjustment of each organism follows from the incorporation of all organisms, however diversified, in a single Nature.

In other words, some kind of pragmatist or functionalist theory of knowledge is presupposed by the very notion of Nature. Nature in turn can plausibly be seen to be an inescapable corollary of the idea of Reason. Reason operates symmetrically and in an orderly way: hence an orderly, rule-bound impersonal system, in other words Nature, is the shadow it casts on the world. So a rationally investigated system inevitably acquires certain formal properties, which are projected onto it by the style of investigation itself. Hence it cannot be cognitively stratified: no part of it may constitute specially weighty evidence, and claim to be a point at which Revelation alters Nature and trumps ordinary, unhallowed facts. So no part of Nature can be sacred – literally or colloquially. In this way, as in some others, Reason cuts its own throat. It demotes itself from the status of a Secular Revelation to one-style-amongst-others. Its conclusions preclude the attribution of a special status, which at the same time it also claims for itself.

But knowledge whose criteria of validity are basically those of adjustment, of pragmatic effectiveness, is therefore inescapably relative. What is functional for one organism in one set of circumstances is not so for another organism in another set. Where is universal truth and universal obligation now? Yet their repudiation was the consequence of working out the implications of ideas or ideals – Nature, Reason – which in themselves seemed impeccably universal and un-opportunistic. They seemed eminently eligible for endorsement and support by a loyal, non-treacherous guild of clerics, which had merely substituted a natural object of reverence for a transcendent one, but had hoped in other ways to carry on As Usual.

In his book, Julien Benda does not offer any real vindication of a Platonic–universalist metaphysic of binding eternal values. The argument, ironically, is implicitly rather pragmatist: unless intellectuals act as if such a metaphysic were indeed valid and binding, and unless they display conspicuous loyalty towards it, certain dire social consequences follow and have already become sadly manifest in modern Europe. If you need proof, says Benda pointing at inter-war Europe, look around yourself, *circumspice*. A most powerful and persuasive argument, this. Murderous political ideologies are supported, shamefully, by treacherous intellectuals. Unfortunately, the argument also happens to be a *pragmatic* one. It appeals to the practical consequences of holding or failing to hold certain views, rather than to their congruence with eternal truth. So we end up with the paradox that he who preaches against the treason of the clerics also commits it in his very sermon; whereas he who preaches that same treason may do so out of an unflinching loyalty to the very values which he is criticizing. It is just because he respects truth, he endorses the conclusion that truth is specific, pragmatic, variable, tied to particular communities or classes. If naturalism and pragmatism are valid, is not a loyal searcher after truth obliged to say so with candour?

This is a fundamental and important point: many of the naturalists, pragmatists, romantics, irrationalists, relativists, who abound so conspicuously in the history of nineteenth and twentieth-century thought, reached their conclusions in an impeccably rational, absolutist, universalist spirit. It was *because* they were so loyal to the old transcendent principle of impartial objectivity that they uncovered something which undermines those principles themselves. Because they were so devoted to the rules of clerkly procedure, they loyally reported their findings. Some, like Nietzsche, fully understood the irony of their own condition.

It is entirely possible to reach the kind of conclusion they reached, to end with a reverence for the particular, the relative, the functional, the instinctive, and to reach that end-point by a path which partakes of none of these traits. It is not only possible but, in the context of the intellectual situation of the age, enormously in character. Those who preached *la trahison* did not commit it; whereas those who preached against it, did.

If the thinkers of the Enlightenment on the whole failed to perceive the strain between their naturalism and their universalism, some of the thinkers of the nineteenth century were aware of it. So as to understand their predicament, let us be the naturalistic devil's advocate. The case can be argued in at least two spheres – that of morals, and that of knowledge. These are in fact the two most important intellectual arenas. Take morals first.

A thinker might well argue as follows. We know now that man is but an animal. We should not be surprised at the vigour of his instinctual drives. Nor should we fail to recognize that it is only these which endow him with vitality, vigour and health. Only the satisfaction of his instinctual needs gives him a genuine gratification. Have puritan and repressive thinkers fulminated against these dark forces within the human psyche, and preached the authority of higher, purer values? Be not deceived. Within the human psyche, there is no counter-force to the dark drives. That which would thwart them in the name of something Higher, is but a devious, disingenuous, twisted form of those very drives themselves, cunningly camouflaged. The dark Will has turned in upon itself. It is no purer than the more candid expressions of our animal nature. It is only more tortured, twisted, cunning, self-thwarting, and more pathogenic. By this argument, the old truths of Romantic literature were fused with the inevitable corollaries of the new information about mankind, relayed by Darwinian biology.

What is the point of upbraiding a thinker of this kind by stigmatizing his doctrine as an instance of the treason of the clerics? The charge only has any force if, first of all, it has been established that what he is asserting is false. And that is by no means obvious. On the contrary: he is only spelling out what seems implied in the evidence before him.

Take the parallel case in the theory of knowledge. American Pragmatism has none of that affinity to Dark Romantic literature which characterizes some of the more sombre philosophy of nineteenth-century Europe. It is, on the contrary, sober and polite and perfectly *salonfähig*. Its case can be stated roughly as follows. Those large, elegant, abstract cognitive structures, associated with transcendental visions, are but the preferred indulgence and joy of genteel souls, sheltered in some cosy rectory. William James said as much, almost in these words. Real, frontiersman knowledge – whether it be on the literal or on the cognitive Frontier – is quite other: rough, piecemeal, untidy, experimental, specific, transient. There is nothing permanent, let alone eternal, about it. The Pragmatist diagnosis of the transcendental illusion is quite different from the Dark-God's denunciation of puritan rectitude, but the basic underlying point is similar. Jamesian Pragmatism castigated grand abstract simplicities in the name of complex tangled earthly realities: an appreciation of the latter was, precisely, its one grand abstract principle! A real practising pragmatist does not elevate his pragmatism into a formal principle: it takes a sincere love of abstract truth to do that.

I have offered simplified versions of the Nietzschean account of morals, and of a Jamesian account of knowledge. Now it would be absurd to pretend that either Friedrich Nietzsche or William James were corrupt servants of some sectional or regional interest, who had betrayed universal values out of some kind of venality or spinelessness. They were unquestionably seekers after truth; one of them was an inwardly tormented one. They were eager to work out what morality or knowledge were or could be, given a naturalistic universe. They followed out the implications of their insights with courage, candour and consistency. If their *conclusions* appear to be in conflict with the universalistic–Platonist picture, their *practice* was an implementation of its requirements. They were inspired by the very ideal whose authority they were undermining. Are we to prohibit such conclusions? Are we to place an interdict on honestly following the wind of argument wherever it may lead? Is prohibition of a given type of conclusions, or of a given type of reasoning, to be an example of respect for truth? In a fascinating footnote in the *Trahison*, Benda half recognizes all this. He observes that though Nietzsche's views were reprehensible, he deserved commendation for his *life*, for the wholehearted manner in which he devoted himself to intellectual concerns. Nietzsche himself had said something similar about Schopenhauer. The real point is not that Nietzsche gave those preoccupations all his time and psychic energy, but that he pursued them with total *integrity*, and that this reflects on the standing of those conclusions. Given the intellectual background situation in which in fact we live, the paradox is that those who teach naturalistic, and hence non-universal, relativistic doctrines, may be impelled to do so by their commitment to the ideal of a single universal truth. It is unfortunate that the truth turns out to be naturalistic. But a loyal seeker after truth bows to logic and evidence, and does not censor the conclusions which honest inquiry imposes on him. Those, on the other hand, who *would* censor such doctrines, thereby display their lack of respect for truth. People may become subjectivists and relativists because respect for truth led them to such conclusions, and others may be absolutist out of opportunism and desire to embrace the comforting conclusion, whether or not it is logically warranted.

Naturalism is not the only point at which this paradox arises. There is also what might be called Hamlet's problem. A firm and resolute defence of those eternal values which, according to Benda, were being betrayed, requires firmness of character, *conviction*. But the cognitive ethic which inspired the modern explosion of knowledge contains at least two provisions incompatible with such firmness. It requires the investigator not to endow any idea with more certainty than the evidence warrants. Even more significantly, it also requires that even seemingly certain, reliable convictions should be probed for weak spots. Descartes codified a cognitive practice embodying similar ideas, though he could nevertheless retain the required firmness in his personal life, by resolving to act in daily life as if the doubts he raised in his theoretical activity did not exist. But such a separation of the theoretical and practical life, which Descartes hoped would only be temporary, can hardly be sustained. Modern morality does in fact accord respect to honest doubt, rather than to ill-founded conviction. Here, once again, by a different route, respect for truth and for the sovereignty of evidence – and are these not eternal values? – at the same time also lead to the weakening of moral fibre and resolution.

Consider a related problem, arising out of the interdependence of all things, and, in particular, the interlocking nature of the modern world. This problem most commonly strikes the modern intellectual in the form – *To Sign or Not To Sign?* He is frequently presented with a protest against some iniquity in a part of the world not close to his own, and requested for his signature in support of the denunciation of the scandal in question. As no man can be fully informed of the merits of all the cases of this kind, to sign without question will inevitably mean occasional support for unworthy or questionable causes. (I understand that when the late Shah's principal police torturer fell out with his master, Bertrand Russell and Jean-Paul Sartre were induced to sign a protest on the man's behalf.) On the other hand, to refrain on principle from supporting any protest whatsoever, is to condone appalling injustices which, at least on some occasions, can be corrected by vigorous protest. It is virtually impossible to formulate any general rule for this kind of case. Our world is now so interdependent that it is impossible to specify the limits of one's responsibility. Who is really guilty of the treason of the clerics – he who never signs, or he who signs any appeal often phrased in plausible (and perhaps question-begging) terminology?

Consider the related problem of 'political realism'. Imagine an oppressive, unrepresentative regime which dominates a given society, but which can, with some justification, invoke the principle of the Lesser Evil. The regime can claim to be committed to averting a far worse evil which looms over the country, and to do it at the least possible cost – in terms of injustice and illiberalism – compatible with the given circumstances. But for us – the apologist of the regime claims – a national calamity would be upon us. We pay a certain price for averting it, but we do all we can to keep that price down to a minimum. A 'realist' will accept the case and co-operate with the regime; an 'irresponsible romantic' will refuse to do so. I am struck by the fact that, in certain countries, there is a kind of spectrum of political positions such that, almost *wherever* a man happens to be located, he feels that the people on one side of him are irresponsible, unrealistic romantics, and those on the other, craven compromisers.

But *if* the irresponsible romantics can combine and form the overwhelming majority, their irresponsible romanticism may, suddenly, become a realistic option. The erstwhile realism will then appear as craven treason. But, in ambiguous and fluctuating circumstances, who can say with confidence which characterization is the correct one? You cannot tell which way the other individuals decide. A big majority of romantics becomes a majority of realists. But if they turn out to be a minority after all, they are irresponsible wreckers of the Least Evil compromise. But quite often, you do not know how the others have chosen when you are making your own decision.

The basic point I have been making is woefully negative and no doubt obvious. The background picture – sociologically, epistemologically, morally – in terms of which the intellectuals have on occasion been excoriated for committing treason is woefully inadequate. It is itself in conflict with those values. It is irresponsibly complacent, self-indulgent and prejudicial. It is not necessarily illegitimate to hold naturalistic theories of knowledge or morality. It is not necessarily wrong to display doubt rather than conviction. It is not necessarily wicked to be less than clear about the limits of one's responsibility. It is not always wrong to be realistic about the situation and to refrain from Quixotry. The recognition of these difficulties is itself a duty. The tacit deployment of a model which fails to do justice to the seriousness of these difficulties is itself a kind of intellectual treason. The strident denunciation of the treason of the clerics, which pretends that our situation is far clearer and unambiguous than in fact it is, is itself a form of betrayal of truth.

The model of the human situation in terms of which the treasonable conduct has been characterized is simply inadequate. The model may have been closer to reality once, but it is very distant from it now. The model assumes, for instance, that the moral agent knows the limits of the community to which he is accountable. This is not so for us: to claim to be concerned with all mankind equally is presumptuous and runs the risk of sacrificing concrete obligations close to home for hypothetical distant ones. But to circumscribe one's moral neighbourhood closely is just as questionable. The boundaries of one's community are not given, but nor is its structure: a man facing a moral dilemma in the context of a given institutional structure had an easier task than one who admits that formally, legally legitimate authorities may on occasion be reprehensible. Neither our moral nor our material environment is free of doubt and ambiguity. Naturalistic ethics, endeavouring to endow our values with an earthly rather than a transcendent basis, are not inherently reprehensible, and cannot be condemned out of hand. It is plausible to hold that our cognitive ethic is such that doubt is a more serious obligation than faith.

Those who have joyfully indulged in what has aptly been called epistemological hypochondria have often, covertly or openly, then made the transition to an unrestrained permissivism: because everything is in question, everything is allowed. A certain methodological antinomianism is rather fashionable. Nothing is further from my intentions. If I underscore the difficulties, it is not with the intention of giving anyone a cognitive or moral *carte blanche*. Quite particularly in the field of factual information about our social and natural environment, the famous under-determination of our vision of things by our database has, like the death of Mark Twain, been grossly, self-indulgently and irresponsibly exaggerated. But the recognition of all this should not lead us to pretend that we live in an easier world, morally or cognitively, than in fact we do. This is the reproach I am addressing to facile versions of the 'treason of the intellectuals' sermon.

I am not saying that the treason of the clerics has never been committed. Deliberate disregard of truth in the interest of loyalty to doctrine is certainly an instance of it. When Jean-Paul Sartre refused to recognize or publicize certain facts about Stalinism, because he considered it more important to protect a French working-class district from despair, he was, unquestionably, committing *la trahison des clercs*. What I *am* saying is that the task of *not* committing is far, far more difficult than an appallingly simplified model of the intellectual's work situation would have us believe. We live in an interlocking world, in which no sphere and no area is insulated. To assess consequences is appallingly difficult. We cannot do everything at once, and must choose our priorities, and do it on the basis of inadequate evidence. To disregard consequences in the name of purity of principle can itself often be a kind of indulgence and evasion. I do not know how this cluster of problems can be handled effectively. But that is no reason for pretending that the problem does not exist, that the path of virtue and loyalty to truth is clearly visible, and that only turpitude prevents us from following it.

5

The Sacred and the National

Conor Cruise O'Brien* is almost uniquely well qualified to write about nationalism and religion. His long involvement with Irish politics, and the outstandingly brave stand he has taken on the Ulster issue, have provided him with ample opportunity and motive to reflect on this topic. His initial literary work was close to the question of how the modern soul experiences religion. His multiple and dramatic involvements in African politics have provided him with intimate and inside knowledge of a whole variety of national and religious conflicts. His reactions are not stereotyped: in Katanga he opposed the secession of a Congolese Ulster, in Biafra he supported the breakaway of a Nigerian one. In Ghana, whilst displaying more sympathy for a tinpot dictator and for his European abettors than they deserved, he nevertheless made a determined stand for academic liberty and integrity against the dictator's attempts to subvert them. Recently, he again displayed his independence in connection with South Africa. It is an impressive record, and given his capacity for both incisive thought and elegant prose even whilst politically engaged, one approaches this book with the highest expectations.

These expectations are fulfilled only in part. This is unquestionably an interesting book, and in parts also a very amusing

* Conor Cruise O'Brien (1988) *GodLand: Reflections on Religion and Nationalism*. Harvard University Press: Cambridge, Mass.

one. But it is also seriously flawed. Conor Cruise O'Brien is not only an analyst, but also a victim, of nationalism. By this I do not mean that he has to live with the knowledge that the IRA may choose to get him. (He has been heard to observe that precautions are useless, because if they do indeed so decide, nothing will stop them executing their decision.) What I do mean is that he has internalized, as initially most of us have, the key nationalist assumption – namely, that the nation, whatever that be, is the natural political unit. Unlike some of us, he has not liberated himself from taking that assumption for granted. He has not come to see that this is a contingent, historically limited condition, and not a universal, self-evident verity. In an earlier work, *To Katanga and Back*, he gave us a fine account of what it feels like to be a member of a non-dominant group. The context of that account made it plain that it was meant to explain his stand in Africa. It may or may not be the case that the African personality (how dated this erstwhile catch phrase now sounds) is moulded by factors similar to those which impinge on an Irish schoolboy in an English school. But that kind of experience does indeed make one sensitive to the significance of nationalist feelings.

Nevertheless some of us, whilst retaining a wholly undiminished sense of the importance of the problem, succeed in liberating ourselves from the social metaphysics of nationalism – the idea that nationality is in the very nature of things the basis of political order. This presupposition pervades our particular world so much that most people presuppose it without realizing that it is indeed a contentious assumption. They deem it as obvious and unproblematic as speaking prose. My own discovery that I was speaking prose, and that forms of discourse other than prose exist, I owe to Elie Kedourie, notwithstanding the fact that I disagree with him totally about the nature of the explanation of the fact which he rightly sees as so contingent. Yet when handling the problem, Conor Cruise O'Brien and Kedourie belong, in a very broad and general sense, to the same camp. They both seek the answer in the history of ideas. There the resemblance ends, though this general similarity is very important. Kedourie locates the origin of nationalism in the high thought of Europe at the turn of the eighteenth and nineteenth centuries, whereas O'Brien goes much further back, with a heavy stress on ancient Israel.

There is, alas, a touch of intellectual autism in O'Brien's thought. Kedourie's name does not appear in the index, and there is no reaction to his ideas. In fact, all participants in what might be called the LSE debate – Kedourie, Minogue, Anthony Smith, Percy Cohen, myself – are ignored. The same fate also befalls others who have contributed to this subject, such as Tom Nairn, Eric Hobsbawm, Michael Hechter, Peter Sugar, Benedict Anderson, Karl Deutsch, Walker Connor, Paul Brass, H. Kohn, J. Brouilly, J. Armstrong and others. Social anthropologists who have written about it, such as E. Wolf, J. Cole, Peter Loizos, Chris Hann, Abner Cohen, Catherine Verdery or Fredrik Barth, are similarly ignored. Hugh Seton-Watson is mentioned once, but only to be laughed at for suggesting that the English do not know nationalism. O'Brien evidently thinks he can crack the nut of nationalism almost unaided. It is also somewhat odd to find a discussion of the role of religion in a society without a mention of the names of Max Weber or Emile Durkheim. Had O'Brien given attention to the latter thinker, he would at least have had to come to terms with the idea that the religious sacralization of the social is of the very essence of religion: hence what is really distinctive in the modern world is not a new and specially destructive intrusion of the sacred, but the fact that it attaches itself to a new kind of social object. The main flaw in O'Brien's argument could however have been avoided if only he had attended to Kedourie's negative point: the problems of social cohesion and that of nationalism are *not* identical.

O'Brien's crucial error is not something which needs to be dug up arduously from his underlying assumptions. It is spelt out loud and clear for all to hear:

It seems impossible to conceive of organised society without nationalism, and even without holy nationalism, since any nationalism which failed to inspire reverence could not be an effective bonding force. (p. 40)

In fact, it is not merely perfectly possible to conceive what O'Brien declares to be inconceivable: it constitutes the normal political condition of most of mankind. Political power may or may not endure without holiness: that is not obvious. But most of the social and political communities which have existed in the course of human history, and which possessed quite enough 'bonding force' to survive for a significant time, were *not* based on the nationalist principle, whether holy or sober. City states, tribal segments, participatory communities of all kinds, were generally much *smaller* than the totality of members of the same culture, or what we now call a 'nation'. At the same time, there were also many *larger* units, dynastic states and empires, whose bounds generally went beyond the limits of what we call a nation. Rulers of such units were not concerned with whether their boundaries transgressed beyond the so to speak ethnographic limits, or even whether they reached them. They were interested in the tribute and labour potential of their subjects, not in their culture. It is only in modern times that this congruence of political and cultural boundaries becomes a matter of pressing concern, and that, consequently, a polity without nationalism becomes well-nigh inconceivable. What we need to explain is how this state of affairs came about – instead of uncritically retrojecting it on to all humanity. O'Brien's egregious generalization of our own distinctive condition paralyses the argument which is based on it. Preoccupied with the interesting question concerning how much holiness is needed for social cohesion, he just assumes that nationalism is also required for this end – which is not the case.

Because O'Brien conflates two things which are inherently distinct (though they are indeed conjoined *in our time*, for reasons which require exploration), he altogether misrepresents his own problem. What he is really investigating is the problem of why some feelings of membership of a political unit become so to speak over-sacralized, over-heated, virulent and dangerous. A good question. But it is not the same question as the one which he also thinks he is pursuing, namely – what is the motive of nationalism? Why do people, *sometimes*, give their loyalty only to units defined by shared culture, in other words, *national* units? Why do identification and loyalty home in, under some conditions, only on collectivities resembling a modern 'nation', i.e. large anonymous assemblies of culturally homogeneous individuals?

Pursuing two distinct issues under the impression that they are but one, O'Brien ends up by stumbling in a conceptual thicket of his own creation. The two questions are quite separate and cut across each other, giving rise to four possibilities: some non-national units are cool and some over-heat, and some national ones are cool and some over-heat. O'Brien is never really clear whether he is concerned with over-heating or with nationalism, or only with over-hot nationalism. The confusion engenders a wobbly, uncertain argument.

This mistake is quite separate from the question concerning whether O'Brien is right in the answer he gives to the question he really is (in the main) pursuing – namely whether, why and to what extent sacralization and emotional excess really are necessary for adequate social bonding. His answer is that they probably are, but that you can have too much of a good thing. Evidently, he hopes that societies may have just enough of it for adequate bonding, but not so much as to indulge in excesses.

For my own part, I am happy to be agnostic about this issue. O'Brien may well be right that some measure of mystical and emotive identification is indispensable, or he may be wrong. It is not self-evident to me that societies may not also be based on fear, inertia, rational self-interest or other principles. But it is at least possible that irrational emotive identification is in the long run indispensable. But even if this is so, it does not in any way follow (nor indeed is it the case) that the object favoured by such murky and half-crazed affection must always be an anonymous set of people sharing the same culture, in other words a nation in the modern sense. Men have often bonded very effectively on the basis of sacralizing concrete specific non-anonymous relationships and loyalties, which failed to expand to the limits of the local culture, or which cut across it. In the past, social structure not culture held society together; but that has now changed. *That* is the secret of nationalism: the new role of culture in industrial and industrialized society.

However, let us reformulate his question for him, so that it corresponds to the problem he is in effect mainly pursuing, rather than to the problem which he thinks he is pursuing. The question then becomes: how is it that, given that men must sacralize their political structures a bit if they are to stick together at all, they sometimes do it to excess, doing each other much harm in the process?

O'Brien begins his treatment of this problem with another muddle. Claiming to correct an un-named recent encyclopedia of political thought (p. 1), he affirms, astonishingly, that nationalism-as-ideology is at present eclipsed by an internationalist and positively anti-nationalist ideology, namely Marxism–Leninism. It is indeed true that Marxism is formally the official doctrine and state religion over extensive parts of the globe. However, at present neither rulers nor subjects in these states have much faith in it, or take it very seriously. It is exceedingly hard to find Marxists in Marxist societies, though it is still possible to find some in non-Marxist ones. The rulers and citizens of Marxist countries continue to pay lip service to it, for a rather good reason. The complex of institutions and ritual affirmation which accompany them, which Marxism had engendered at a time when it *was* still taken seriously – i.e. a stagnation-age ago – are the only barriers to political chaos. This chaos would be provoked, above all, by the genuine strength of nationalism. Wishing to avoid such chaos, they stick to the only language and set of institutions available. They wouldn't now dream of embracing Marxism if only they could go back to the starting point, but they can't. They have to cope with their mess as best they can, with the institutional and ritual tools which happen to be to hand.

It is precisely this kind of pragmatic motivation which makes me sceptical about O'Brien's contention that society cannot be kept going by prudential considerations, unaided by sacralization. It would seem that custom and cold prudence can keep a society going. Still, I would not wish to dogmatize about this: O'Brien may be proved right on this point, if it turns out that a new set of institutions cannot be erected without a new faith. We shall see. But at present, for instance, the current ruler of the USSR makes it plain that he is committed to the perpetuation of a Leninist single party rule, not because he believes in it as a unique and universally valid solution, but because in the contingent historical situation which has arisen, there is no other way. *Tak istoricheski sluchilos*. (It just so happened.) I have listened to Gorbachev's speeches on Soviet TV with great attention, and it is quite obvious to me that this is the message he is trying to put over. Never perhaps has Leninism proper been so summarily dismissed. His own rather curious Leninism is pragmatic and tied to given specific circumstances. He wishes to use a disciplined monopolistic avant-garde party to bring about a transformation which that party had originally been designed to prevent, in circumstances in which that transformation is menaced, above all, by *nationalism*. To describe such a situation as the eclipsing of nationalist ideology by a Marxist internationalist one seems to me bizarre.

Having failed to make a distinction which does need to be made (between the sacralization and the nationalization of politics), O'Brien tries to make a distinction which cannot be made: between nationalism as an ideology and as a sentiment. (It is this which enables him to make the astounding statement that nationalism as an ideology is eclipsed, by allowing it to be strong as a sentiment.) But nationalism is not a shapeless free-floating unspecific unfocused feeling, like some nameless elusive *Angst*. Its object is normally only too sharply defined, as the love of certain categories of people, and the detestation of others. This cognitive element, the determination of the object of the feeling, pervades the sentiment, is part of it, and constitutes its 'ideological' core, and it is in no way 'eclipsed'. God help you if you find yourself with the wrong face, colour or accent in a mob possessed by nationalist hysteria.

There is an element of truth in this muddle. It is indeed the case that nationalism as an elaborated intellectual *theory* is neither widely endorsed, nor of high quality, nor of any historic importance. The sharp delineation of the object of nationalist feeling is not the work of formal theory at all, it is not produced by the historic accumulation of premises pointing a certain way, but,

on the contrary, by very concrete earthy social situations. It is for
this reason that I am allergic to the history-of-ideas approach to
nationalism (shared by O'Brien with Kedourie, for all the differences in their implementation of it). Given O'Brien's evident
awareness of the eclipse of this doctrinal aspect of nationalism,
it is all the harder to understand why he adopts the general
strategy which seeks the roots of nationalism in the intellectual
development of mankind.

But although social factors are acknowledged in a piecemeal
kind of way, it is this intellectualist approach which gives the
argument its backbone. In the beginning was the Word. 'Nationalism, as a collective emotional force in our culture, makes its
first appearance, with explosive impact, in the Hebrew Bible' (p.
2). Political sacralization began when the deity linked itself to a
specific land and people. Christianity dissolved these links, both
by abrogating the boundary around the chosen people, and by
turning its back on literally terrestrial politics. O'Brien repeats
the jibe made by the Saudi delegate to the United Nations, noting
that the God of the New Testament, unlike that of the Old, loses
interest in real estate. But this flight into the skies is reversed
once again when Christianity is adopted by the Roman Empire.

> So the Roman patria joins the Jewish Promised Land, and fuses
> it with the sky. (p. 13)

The subsequent story as told by O'Brien is too complex to be
summarized, but the central point is that the re-terrestrialization
of religion, begun by the Romans, is pushed further by the Reformation. For one thing the Protestants were more serious about
the Old Testament, and so the deity returned to its earlier real-
estate vocation. For another, any nation which came down firmly
on one side or another of the great religious divide, henceforth
experienced a powerful injection of religious feelings into ethnic
ones, and vice versa. This naturally leads O'Brien to modern
nationalism and the intrusion of religious passion into politics,
which he identifies with it. He is of course entirely convincing
when he talks about Irish nationalism:

Irish nationalist ideology, Irish Republicanism . . . beneath an increasingly perfunctory pseudosecular cover, is Irish Catholic holy
nationalist. (p. 39)

I would only add that my own reading of Irish nationalist material suggests to me that the verbiage is often not merely secular,
but also Marxist. But it is indeed pure verbiage. This hardly
allows one to say that Marxist internationalism 'eclipses' nationalism. O'Brien has a much clearer perception of ideological
realities under the surface when it comes to Ireland than when
he deals with the USSR. Wholly convincing about Ireland, interesting but paradox-prone about France, England, America and
Africa, he is not to be taken seriously when talking about the
Soviet Union.

It is after this that O'Brien really clarifies his own position on
nationalism and religion. Religion/nationalism is indispensable
for social cohesion:

Would rationality, self-interest, and pragmatism continue to hold
you together, or would you burst apart, once you had lost the
common bond of national religion? My guess is that you would
burst apart. (p. 41)

The 'you' in the quote is his American audience.

But enough is enough. O'Brien constructs an interesting scale
of nationalisms: chosen nation (but liable to receive a divine
notice to quit); holy nation (chosen, but with tenure); and dei-
fied nation. The first two at least remain under divine scrutiny,
though in the second case, the deity has deprived itself of sanc-
tions. In the third version the nation deifies itself and escapes
all restraint. It becomes a self-vindicating standard of all holiness. O'Brien has some interesting things to say about the recent
oscillations of the needle which indicates the location of the USA
along this spectrum. (But it is odd that someone discussing the
Americanization of religion and the sacralization of America should
not refer to the work of W. Herberg.)

He also believes that the American Revolution was primarily a

Protestant movement. He would have the colonists more upset by George III's flirtation with his newly acquired Catholic Canadian subjects than by his attempts at absolutism. Popery disturbed them more than Taxation without Representation. This thesis leads him to some candidly avowed difficulties when it comes to dealing with the colonists' Franco-Spanish alliance and other accommodations. But if American nationalism was Protestant in its origins, it became more ecumenically Christian thanks to the efforts of Cardinal Spellman, Senator McCarthy and John F. Kennedy:

> McCarthyism was an engine for the social promotion of Catholics in America and the promotion of Irish Catholics in particular. McCarthy, backed by Spellman, conveyed to millions of non-Catholic anti-Communist Americans the novel idea that Catholics were a specially reliable, and especially tough, breed of anti-Communist . . . Personally, I believe that without Joe McCarthy's crusade in the 1950s, John F. Kennedy could not have been elected in 1960. (p. 36)

In brief, the book contains an interesting discussion of whether and to what extent the polity must also be religious, bedevilled by the gratuitous assumption that it must *in any case* be national.

One of the many points where this comes out is in an interesting passage which in effect turns Spinoza into a proto-Zionist. Spinoza, he says (p. 49), 'comes very close to asserting the identity of nationalism and true religion', and would seem to be on the verge of dancing the *hora* in a Kibbutz. The evidence adduced suggests nothing of the kind. It shows Spinoza endorsing a Hobbesian theory of politics. Without the state, all else goes. But there is nothing in this to make the state *national*. What *is* true is that Spinoza, and the Enlightenment after him, having decreed that there is but one world, can no longer revere the Other one. Henceforth, obligation, identity and loyalty must have mundane bases. This means that men can only sacralize this world or within this world, if indeed they are to sacralize at all. (We have seen that O'Brien believes, with some regret perhaps, that indeed they must.) But the inference from this to the conclusion that we must sacralize the *nation* follows only if one assumes that within this world, there is no other political candidate. This is a preposterous and unwarranted restriction of the range of candidates. O'Brien admits that in theory, humanity as a whole might provide an alternative object of reverence. Then, verging on contradiction, he both dismisses this option because this colourless abstraction has little appeal, and notes that in any case, dreadful things have also been committed in its name. Can a temptation be both feeble and yet powerful enough to seduce men into committing terrible atrocities?

But the main point remains. The argument-by-elimination, which suggests that once deities and kings are de-sacralized, then nations must inherit their aura, simply does not follow. There are other options. The real problem in understanding nationalism is: why is it that, of the many things found within this world, which in the past often have attracted devotion and loyalty, it is precisely large, anonymous categories of people-sharing-the-same-culture, which capture most of the available political affect? An argument from allegedly manifest elimination provides a facile and invalid distraction from the main task of tackling the problem of nationalism.

There is also a methodological problem which faces O'Brien. It is hard to see how the rather *simpliste* argument from elimination, which turns nations into the residual legatees of sacredness when the gods have gone, is compatible with the complex, not to say tortuous route by which it is claimed that we have reached the age of nationalism. Either of the two arguments, the complex and the simple, would seem to render to other one otiose. If we have no other option anyway, why bother with the obscure by-ways of old theologies which may have led us where we are? Or if, on the other hand, we did indeed arrive in our present impasse by so tortuous a path, then surely there must have been many unused turnings, which would have taken us some place else, had we but taken them – so that our options must be that much more numerous. I happen to believe that the Tortuous Path approach is inherently misguided. The argument by Elimination just happens to be mistaken.

This methodological difficulty really comes home to roost in the final chapter, though it is mentioned much earlier (p. 8). In the final passages, O'Brien assures Americans, quite rightly, that Third World revolutionaries are nationalists first and Marxists (at most) second. (He ignores Roman Szporluk's recent book on Marxism and nationalism which argues, convincingly to my mind, that this has long been true of most Marxists.) But how can nationalism be so well diffused and yet be rooted in the Abrahamic tradition? How come it has sprung up in societies not pervaded by the Old Testament? This wildfire spread is even odder than Kedourie's diffusionist doctrine that nationalism is a virus conceived in the mind of Kant and a few other thinkers, which then infects the masses the world over with catastrophic speed and effect.

O'Brien notices this problem rather early, but tries to shrug it off first by suggesting that authors other than himself should explore the roots of nationalism in them foreign parts, and then by adding that in any case, nationalism is specially strong amongst *us*. (That was in another country, and besides, the wench is dead.) But this turns the simultaneous emergence of nationalism in other countries, due to causes yet to be explored, into an astonishing coincidence. The highly specific outcome of a long and very complicated development, stretching from the Old Testament to the present, *also* appears as the end product of some other and quite different developments, and very nearly at the very same time. Such a remarkable convergence of otherwise very distinct and independent paths makes too great a demand on one's credulity.

In the final part of the book, there are also some more specific slips, rather surprising in one so deeply involved in Africa. The Somalis are accused of wishing to revise African boundaries in the light of 'tribal factors' (p. 79). Tribalism is indeed important in Somali *internal* politics (though officially proscribed and denied, in brazen defiance of the facts of the case); but when it comes to the issue of Somalia's *external* borders, the Somalis have as good a case for being treated as a nation, and not a tribe, as any European state–nation. O'Brien here seems to descend to the 'irregular noun' practice, in which other people's nationalisms are called tribalism.

The key factors which have contributed to the vigorous crystallization of Somali nationalism are precisely those which O'Brien singles out in his discussion of the role of the Reformation in the genesis of European nationalism: a cultural boundary is confirmed and exacerbated by the superimposition of a religious one. The Somalis are *the* representatives of Islam in the Horn of Africa, in opposition to Christians and pagans, so that faith and ethnicity reinforce each other. O'Brien also makes the strange assertion to the effect that Somalis put forward territorial claims against the Sudan, in the hope of re-incorporating compatriots located in that country. In fact, there is no Somali population anywhere near the Sudan, and the Somalis make no such claim. The five stars on the Somali flag stand for territories in Djibuti, Ogaden, Kenya, plus the two colonial Somalilands (British and Italian), but not for any part of the Sudan, as O'Brien claims.

There is another strange and more general error (p. 72):

Soviet nationalism – multi-national nationalism – has been far more successful than is generally recognised ... In practice, it culminated in Soviet nationalism, which successfully combined differentiated cultural nationalisms with one overriding political nationalism. What is important about Marxism within this system is not that it is believed to be universally valid but that it is the national religion of the Soviet Union.

Try telling this to anyone in Tallin, Riga, Vilnius, Erevan, Tbilissi, Baku or Sochi. This was already a very strange thing to say in 1987, when these lectures were delivered, and it is of course known to be absurd now. Marxism is indeed the official doctrine and language of the Soviet Union (O'Brien is right to that extent), but it is no longer a religion with the sacralizing potential which the argument requires. Rather, it is an institution, in some ways resembling Anglicanism. O'Brien laughs at Seton-Watson for saying that the English are innocent of nationalism. But note that on O'Brien's own argument, they ought indeed to be unable to have any. Their national church does not sacralize their nationality. An Englishman need not be an Anglican, and episcopalians need not be English. O'Brien, who calls the British monarch a 'theological schizophrenic', knows all about this. It used to be said that the national church sacralizes the Tory party, but that link has recently become very tenuous, to say the least. Sacralization was indeed attempted by the *extremists*, as O'Brien reports, but the job of the official church was precisely to keep down such extremism, to combat 'enthusiasm'. Just as the monarchy is valued above all for preventing the sacralization of operational politics, so the church is valued for preventing the sacralization of anything else.

In the USSR, Marxism is now as it were Anglicanized. It is upheld, in as far as it is, not because there is any inclination to revere it – there is no 'enthusiasm' – but because it is the only barrier available against the explosion of specific nationalisms (including a Great Russian one). I would hardly call this an eclipse of nationalism ideology by a Marxist one. The difference is that whereas the Anglicans did for a long time have extremists on their left to worry about, the CPSU (B) has none to speak of, at any rate in that direction. Whereas the Anglican *zastoi* was troubled by noncomformists and Methodists, no *Sovietski* John Wesley arose to disturb the long sleep of the Brezhnev period. It might all have been different if only *perestroika* had begun in the course of the first, Krushchevian Thaw, when there was still some faith left. Now it is too late. The few old believers who are left are bitter about that lost opportunity. They weren't allowed to get on the right course then, and can no longer do so now. As for the existence of that overriding Soviet nationalism . . . it resolutely refuses to exist and be sacralized, despite all efforts. There are some *inter*nationalists who would like it to exist so as to diminish strife, but that is another matter.

All of this shows, once again, that the problem of nationalism is not about the intrusion of the sacred into the political (simply assumed to be inherently ethnic), but about the sacralization-proneness and salience of nations, *in the modern world*. They attract sacralization, and other real or potential political objects do not. The idea that the trouble arises from the excessive political intrusion of the sacred as such, but for which there would be nothing to worry about, is of course natural in an Irish context. It may well be true in Ireland: the *Gaeltacht* on its own would cause no problems, any more than it does in Scotland. Without a sacralized religious differentiation, there is no real cultural boundary in Ireland. But this point cannot be generalized for the world at large.

6

A Non-nationalist Pole

Bronislaw Malinowski's last book, written in the early forties, not long before he died, *Freedom and Civilisation*, consisted of the reflections of the leading anthropologist of the time on the world at war and the prospects of a post-war settlement. The distinction of the author might in itself give the book a certain mild claim on our attention, but one might well suspect that its importance would not go much further. Are not these political reflections now sadly dated? Malinowski, one might say, had good liberal instincts by the standards of the time, but that time is now long past.

The winds of change had scarcely begun to blow then, and in the meantime they have blown away much of what he still very much took for granted. He was no doubt much concerned with the culture and well-being of the natives, but in a patronizing manner that did not really challenge the basic assumptions of the colonial system. Whilst retaining the assumption that the colonial peoples must be governed from above – though this was to be done with an understanding and utilization of their own institutions – his thought also seems pervaded by an even more dated League of Nations idealism. An academic dreamer blended with a crypto-Blimp – does he really have anything to teach us? Ought we not simply to treat the book as the reflections of a man on a topic on which his distinctive genius did not shine: interesting as evidence of his personal views but not really a contribution to the advancement of thought?

Such a reaction might be natural, but it would also be mis-guided. Malinowski's ideas in the field, far from being merely a set of notions mildly ahead of their own time but badly dated in ours, in fact represent or express a really radical alternative to the way things have gone. The political thought systematized in his last book and found scattered throughout his work constitutes an excellent starting point for the exploration of this alternative. Moreover, it has now become possible, thanks to researches by Polish scholars into Malinowski's youth, to understand the roots of his vision in the intellectual and political turmoil in Cracow and Zakopane at the turn of the century. These findings are at long last accessible in English (as *Malinowski Between Two Worlds* [Cambridge: Cambridge University Press]), and the contentions in this essay are based upon them.

Perhaps one should begin with the theme of decolonization. Since 1945, the political decolonization of the world has largely been accomplished. Discontinuous seaborne empires, at any rate, have become politically unacceptable and have in the main been dismantled. There are two reasons for this. The colonial nations themselves have come to feel guilty about colonialism, and a significant proportion of their citizens were eager to dismantle the empires. Secondly, the cold war between the blocs and the nuclear stalemate have meant that the major international con-flict is being fought out by proxy. Overtly dominated colonies, especially when not territorially continuous with the centre of power, constitute a disastrous point of weakness for any state that tries to retain them. When sustained by the enemies of the power in question, resistance movements can impose an intoler-able strain on the resources and morale of a would-be persistent colonial power. There is no point in trying to assess the relative importance of guilt-ridden good will and pressurized fear and self-interest in the abandonment of empire. Both played their part, and no doubt the proportions varied from case to case.

The anti-colonial moral intuition can be formulated in terms of two propositions: (1) the inequality of colonizer and colonized is

morally intolerable; (2) therefore, the colonized must be decolonized, granted political independence, so as to become similar to
the colonizers – and as fast as possible. Anti-colonialists have not
distinguished between these two claims. They have generally considered them to be one single claim – or thought that the second
followed, obviously and inevitably, from the first. *It does not.* The
two ideas are wholly independent. It is possible to affirm the first
and yet be in no way committed to the second. This was in fact
at the core of Malinowski's position: moreover, it has some merits
and deserves, at the very least, elaboration if not assent.

It is possible to repudiate the inequality of colonist and colonizer
with passion and yet feel no need whatever to decolonize. Moral
symmetry – though this does not seem to have occurred to many
people – can just as effectively be secured by the very opposite:
not by decolonizing the colonized but by colonizing the colonists. The colonized ought never to have been granted independence, but the colonizers should have been *deprived* of it. This is
not just a logical point; it has a great deal of substance.

The case against decolonizing is that the Africans, Asians and
Oceanians who were being decolonized are not fit to rule themselves. This is unquestionably the case. They are just as unfit to
rule themselves as are the Poles, the English and everyone else.
No nation is fit to rule itself. Generally speaking, what is it that
self-governing nations do? They fight each other, and they op-
press their own minorities and hamper – if not worse – the free
expression of their culture. In a very significant proportion of
cases, moreover, self-governing nations are such only in the sense
that they are not governed by members of some *other* nation.
That does not save them from dictators of their own ilk.

The next step in the argument requires one to specify what it
is that government is meant to do. Why was it instituted amongst
men? What are the functions of government? Every schoolboy in
Cracow knows the answer, though strangely enough there are
many professors of political science in the West who don't get it
right. The basic roles of government are simple: (1) to keep
nations from fighting each other; (2) to protect national cultures,
which alone give meaning and richness to life; and (3) to protect

nations from the Russians. Governments sometimes also do other things, but that is generally a mistake. These three really essential functions, however, were on the whole rather well performed by the Habsburg empire, for which Malinowski had an undisguised admiration and affection. Many others in Cracow and elsewhere have come to feel the same: better Franz Josef than Josef, as you might say.

Here we come to the heart of his political thought, where we find a partly implicit but pervasive and dominant triple equation: Habsburg empire = League of Nations = indirect rule. The first step in the equation was in fact explicitly affirmed by Malinowski. The second can be understood if we consider the nature of indirect rule as practised early in this century in Cracow as well as in Kano. Normally it is held to be the use of indigenous institutions by the colonial power with a view to greater effectiveness and diminution of both offence and expense. But this is not its essence. What really gave indirect rule the attractiveness that it indisputably had for many who were involved in it was that it satisfied the basic requirement of the colonial rulers – that they should reserve for themselves certain crucial powers whilst at the same time preserving a very great deal of the indigenous culture. Indirect rule preserves the dances and the ceremonials, the music and the poetry – whether in the literal sense or in the structure of personal relations – that made up the old local culture. Direct rule, by contrast, erodes and obliterates them.

Malinowski was no fool, and he had no illusion that indirect colonial rule really preserved the institutions and cultural traits in their original form. The sheer fact that they were being used for a new end inevitably transformed them. But this cultural change did at least ensure the perpetuation of a distinctive culture as a vital and functioning thing and not as a museum specimen.

The notion of culture is central to Malinowskian anthropology, which sees men not as economists see them, as pursuers of atomized aims by given means, but as creatures who find their fulfilment and satisfaction in living out, dancing out a culture. Malinowski was a cultural nationalist, not merely on behalf of his own nation but on behalf of all of them. But he was not a political nationalist and emphatically did not follow Hegel in supposing that nations only found their fulfilment and maturity in possessing their own state. Their fulfilment lay in their culture, not in their state, which they could well do without. Possessing it only led them into temptation to which they generally succumbed.

A social anthropologist is unlikely to commit the howler of supposing that only state-endowed groups can possess a rich, intricate and fulfilling culture. But how could that culture find the necessary protection and political maintenance without the state? Answer: by indirect rule. That is precisely what indirect rule is: cultural autonomy without political independence. And who is to be the power wielding this indirect rule? Answer: a League of Nations with teeth. We know it can be done: we know that nations can be endowed with the conditions for a full cultural expression without at the same time being allowed to inhibit the expression of others and to fight them. We know this, or at any rate Malinowski knew it, because this is precisely what the Habsburg empire had done. The famous remark to the effect that it was a prisonhouse of nations is rubbish: it was a kindergarten of nations.

Of course, some places lend themselves to indirect rule better than others. Northern Nigeria, for instance, was very well suited to it and continued to practise it even after Independence. Once this kind of Habsburg-style super-League was installed generally, it would in all probability also work exceedingly well in England. The League commissioner, perhaps a minor Habsburg archduke, would work discreetly from some functional but unostentatious secretariat, located in a new edifice in some anonymous London suburb – say Neasden. An architect in the Bauhaus tradition would be commissioned to design it. All ritual and symbolic activities, on the other hand, would continue to be based on Buckingham Palace. Thus the English would be emotionally spared any visible, let alone conspicuous, externalization or expression of their diminished sovereignty.

All institutions whose primary or sole role is the maintenance and servicing of the national culture – the British Council, the

National Trust, the Church of England and so on – would function as before, seldom if ever in any way hampered by the suitably distant and tactful commissioner/archduke. Ritual and symbolic life would become much more, not less, active; a cultural effervescence would more than compensate for diminution of political independence and of its symbolic tokens, such as an independent rate of inflation. Perhaps one could hope for a literary flowering comparable to that of pre-Independence Poland and Ireland or post-Independence Czechoslovakia. Elsewhere, say, in Poland, the advanced erosion of ancient institutions might require either more direct rule or the invention of new institutions, complete with attribution of antiquity. None of this should present much of a problem.

The vision, inspired by a conflation of the best elements in Habsburg and colonial rule, has both its attractions and its weaknesses. The universal protection of cultural autonomy, combined with political constraint imposed by a benevolent centre, must clearly appeal to an age such as ours, which suffers from the opposite condition – political independence blended with dreary cultural standardization. Some of the problems faced by the vision are practical: where would this central superpower, the new League, come from, and whence would it derive both its moral legitimacy and the effective coercive power that it would certainly need to work properly? I have no answer to this question, and I don't suppose Malinowski had one either.

There is also a theoretical problem: Malinowski saw the fulfilment of men in their distinctive cultures, but he also had to face and explain the fact that some cultures are authoritarian, non-participatory and destructive of others. This he found difficult to justify logically. If one validates values by an appeal to culture and its role in human life, it is hard at the same time also to explain bad traditions as the fruits of a bad culture. If culture *as such* is good, the central condition of human fulfilment, it is not clear how there can also be good and bad cultures.

Malinowski's politics were, however, deeply congruent with his anthropological vision. In his anthropology, he had rejected not the claim that evolution had occurred but the claim that it was relevant: the explanation of institutions was to be in terms of their synchronic function, not of their place in an evolutionary sequence. The place in the evolutionary sequence explains nothing, and it does not *justify* anything either. Thus his politics resembled his methodology. But he differed profoundly from the evolutionists, for whom the distinction between good and bad cultures is intimately and essentially linked to the location of a culture on the evolutionary ladder. They ranked cultures by their 'level', and they linked both explanation and validation to evolutionary sequences. Malinowski did neither: there was good and bad among the early and primitive, and there was good and bad among the late and complex. Evolutionary ranking was neither here nor there. Though he may have been a kind of crypto-Blimp in wishing everyone without exception to be subject to indirect rule, he was entirely free from the vainglorious nineteenth-century Europocentric linkage of moral and political virtue to evolution, conceived as finding its culmination in *us*.

The image of a wholly colonized, rather than wholly decolonized, world, in which all cultures are free to express themselves and protected but none is endowed with independent destructive political power, is attractive. It may not be feasible, or may not be feasible yet. If world government ever comes, it ought surely to have this form. Thinking about its conditions and consequences would do us no harm; and Malinowski had already begun to do it in the early forties.

7

Kemalism

Turkey has a special claim on the attention of anyone concerned with the future of liberal societies, with economic development or with Islam. Turkey is located, so to speak, at the intersection of these three great issues. Each of these topics has been of interest to me for a long time, so it was inevitable that I should give some thought to Turkey, notwithstanding my lack of any real, specialized knowledge.

The belief is widespread in the West that few liberal democracies can be found in Asia and Africa, and that the prospects for their emergence or survival are poor. Yet there are three very important states in Asia – Japan, India and Turkey – which continue to exemplify some of the fundamental features valued by Western liberals: constitutionalism and genuine elections. Their existence in some measure compensates for the pessimism inspired by socialist fundamentalism (recently toned down) in China, and Muslim fundamentalism in Iran.

In this trio of liberal hopefuls, Turkey stands out for two reasons. Paradoxically, constitutional elective government is both intermittent and deep-rooted. Secondly, Turkey was never colonized or occupied. Indian constitutionalism, though never yet interrupted by military or ideocratic rule, can be attributed to the institutions bequeathed by the British Raj. In Japan, democracy can be explained by the American occupation, though perhaps it was reinforced by the subsequent economic miracle. Turkey on the other hand can claim that its commitment to modern political ideas owes nothing to alien imposition, and everything to an endogenous development. Turkey chose its destiny. It achieved political modernity: it was not thrust upon it.

The fact that elective and constitutional government is periodically interrupted – one is inclined to say punctuated – by military coups, can be interpreted, from a liberal viewpoint, in both a favourable and an unfavourable light. It does of course mean that liberal democracy has not had an easy ride. But it *also* means that the commitment to constitutional government is deep enough to ensure that it is eventually restored. It is an old and hallowed common custom in other lands for any colonel or general who takes over power so as to save the nation, to announce that he is only doing so as a temporary emergency measure: civilian rule will be restored at the first opportunity. He, the colonel or general, has no more ardent wish than to hand over power again, and return to the barracks. The endearing eccentricity of the Turkish military appears to be that they actually mean it. In due course, they do actually implement the promise, without needing the encouragement of a military defeat. There is the old joke, Mark Twain's I think, who said that giving up smoking is easy: he had done it so many times. The Turkish officer class can say that it can demonstrate its great commitment to democracy: it has restored it so often. Others only abolish democracy once: the Turkish army has done so repeatedly.

Facetious though the argument sounds, it does possess some force, at any rate to a superficial observer such as myself. The first Turkish paradox is that the Kemalist tradition contains a deep commitment to Westernization, and that Westernization is conceived in nineteenth-century terms. It is held to include the values and institutions believed at the time to contain the secret of Western economic and military power. Yet the ultimate guardian and guarantor of those values, firmly determined to step in whenever they are seriously threatened, is an institution which by its own function, tradition and lifestyle has little elective affinity with them – *the army*. The Turks are *successful* Decembrists – and the Decembrist rising has become a permanent institution.

A further important feature of the Turkish way to modernization is that its ideology is not orchestrated in any excessive detail.
Whatever influence Durkheim or any other Western thinker may
have had on the Turkish intelligentsia, there is no highly articulated *Sunna* of modernity. This conspicuously distinguishes Turkey
from countries which modernized 'under the banner of Marxism'. There is a certain resemblance to Brazil, with its loose
paternalistic military positivism. So the commitment to modernity may be deep, but it is not rigidly tied to any elaborate and
constraining doctrine. No doubt there is a corpus of Kemalist
hadith, but it is not specific enough to prejudge too many options
in the Turkish path of development.

One has the impression that the Turkish commitment to
modernization of the polity and society has, or initially had, both
an Ottoman and a Koranic quality. The new faith, like the old,
is linked to the state, constitutes its legitimation and is itself in
turn justified by the strength which it bestows on the state. The
state maintains a certain detachment from society, not so much,
one suspects, because of any influence of Adam Smith and his
followers, as through a kind of revival of the Circle of Equity: the
state is there to be strong, maintain order, enforce good and
suppress evil, not to meddle in production. The *raya* is there to
produce enough to keep the state in the style to which it is
accustomed, and to obey. As Paul Stirling had pointed out, during
the early decades of its existence, the Kemalist republic had
transformed the upper levels of society, the state and the higher
intellectual or ideological institutions, but left the mass of the
peasantry largely untouched.[1] It was only later that urban growth
and migration to the towns meant that the great changes also
involved the rest of the population.

I well remember my first visit to Turkey, which took place
some time in the 1960s. The occasion was a conference, to
which I was invited somewhat to my surprise. It was organized
by a political science association, and was to be devoted to the

---

[1] Paul Stirling, 'Social change and social control in republican Turkey', in
*Turkiye Is Bankasi. Papers and Discussions: International Symposium on Ataturk
(1981)*, 1982.

subject of religion and its socio-political role. The pre-conference specification of the general theme was abstract and anodyne: religion is an important social institution, and it behoves us to understand its social impact, the conference blurb informed us. The programmatic notice of the conference was somewhat longer than this, and more academese in tone, but that was its gist. No one could have dissented from its innocuous claims, or have learnt much from them. But when I came to the conference, the preoccupations of its Turkish participants were far more sharply defined and focused, and I learnt a very great deal from them. Their concern could also be summed up but briefly, and vigorously: how on earth do we stop the Anatolian peasantry, and the petty bourgeoisie of the towns, from voting for the party, or for any party, which chooses to play the religious card? That was the problem.

The Turkish elite evidently faced an interesting dilemma. The Kemalist heritage of firm Westernization included both democracy and secularism. The underlying syllogism had been: the West is secular and democratic. The West is strong. We must be strong. So we must be democratic and secular. We must be democratic *so as* to be strong (for the democratic West is strong). So the carrier and guarantor of national strength, the army, must also watch over the preconditions of strength. If those preconditions contain elements *contrary* to a military and hierarchical organization, the army, in its loyal and disciplined way, will enforce them all the same.

So far so good. But what if it turns out that you cannot, at least in this particular country, be both secular *and* democratic? What if, as soon as you have genuine elections, an excessive proportion of the electorate votes for the party with a religious appeal? What if subsequently, this victorious party endangers the Kemalist heritage itself? What then? If secular democracy votes itself out, what is to be done?

Evidently those who had initially forged the tradition had not fully anticipated this problem, and had failed to prepare a good answer for it. No very good theoretical solution is available, though some intellectuals are evidently trying to work one out. But a kind of solution was achieved in political praxis. I noted what the solution was: and no doubt, in my ignorance of the details and the nuances, I may have simplified and travestied it.

In essence this solution seemed to me to run as follows: we *shall* hold genuine elections. If the result goes against us, and confers electoral victory on the religious opportunists, or those wishing to pander to them, we shall loyally accept the verdict. For a time, anyway. But if the victors go too far, the army, as the guardian of the Kemalist *Sunna*, will step in, and hang the principal traitor to the Tradition. But our commitment to the Tradition will remain firm, and after a while, we shall re-institute civilian rule, elections and the lot. If the previous scenario then repeats itself, we'll have to repeat our intervention as well. Let no one have any doubts about that. There is a monument to the army in Ankara in the form of a giant bayonet rampant. If I read the symbolism correctly, it says, loud and clear: if the *raya* and/ or its elected representatives go too far, we shall step in, and you know exactly what we shall do. We shall also do it if extremists, whether of religion or of Leftism, or both of them, go beyond the limits. We have done it before and we shall do it again. You have been warned. We are the Guardians of the Tradition.

The consequence seems to be a new version of cyclical politics, though rather different from the old famous theory of Ibn Khaldun. Whenever the popular backsliding from the Tradition exceeds permissible limits, a Kemalist purification from above is re-imposed by the guardians of the national tradition. As both principal partners to this situation are perhaps driven by an inner compulsion to go on behaving the way they do, there may be no reason why this pendulum should not swing forever.

The conference at which I made these no-doubt superficial observations took place so long ago that some of the *ansar* of Ataturk were still alive and present. From them and their entourage, one could obtain some sense of the moral climate of the first generation of Young Turks. The discussion turned to a newspaper announcement, published by a set of prominent intellectuals, shortly after one of the military coups. The announcement explained why the signatories held the coup to be necessary and legitimate. A person reading a paper at the conference noted that this pronouncement was a kind of Kemalist *fatwa*. Someone else promptly criticized this view with vigour, pointing out that it was not a real *fatwa*, because . . . I forget the precise reasons why it was not fully up to the standards of a true *fatwa*, but the reasons were numerous, precise, and formulated with a legal verve and formality. The person raising these objections was obviously not merely an *alim* of Kemalism, but equally, an erstwhile *alim* proper: he was well equipped to supply a full, detailed, comprehensive and reliable account of the theology and jurisprudence relevant to the notion of a *fatwa*. The episode illustrated and confirmed something I had come to suspect: the spirit in which Kemalism was formulated and upheld was, at any rate in the first generation, a kind of perpetuation of High Islam. The spirit was projected onto a new doctrine. The content was new, but the form and spirit were not.

After the conference we were taken on an excursion into the countryside. It was pleasant to discover the melancholy enchantment of the Anatolian plateau and highlands. From the viewpoint of one's political initiation, the highlight of the trip came with a visit to a kind of educational club in a large village or small town – I forget what these centres are called, but I later read a scholarly article about them by an Israeli Turcologist.[2] We had a long conversation with the devoted and hard-working man who ran this centre. He was a committed missionary of the secular progressive faith amongst the pagans of Anatolia. Obviously a devoted man, he would not fail to perform his duty, whatever the odds, and whatever the discouragement. But he was evidently much saddened by his overall experience, and sustained in the exercise of his calling only by an inner firmness, and not by any success or external encouragement. However cogent and lucid the Enlightenment which he brought to the villagers, it struck no real echo in their hearts, and had little permanent impact. They would listen, but give them half a chance, he said,

[2] Ehud Houminer, 'The People's House in Turkey', *Asian and African Studies*, Annual of the Israel Oriental Society, vol. 1, 1965, Jerusalem, p. 80.

and off they'll be on the *hajj*. No doubt many earlier missionar-
ies, for instance purist Muslims endeavouring to wean rustics
from their local shrines, had felt much the same.

All that was a generation ago. The *ansar* of Kemal are no
longer with us. The most recent coup was triggered off by a
situation which was no mere replay of the overthrow of Menderes:
the crucial justification was not so much a suspected betrayal of
the Kemalist heritage, as the inability of a civilian government to
contain an appalling escalation of violence from the extremes of
left and right. I remember walking in Ankara on the day of the
funeral of the assassinated no. 2 of the Rightist Colonel Turkes:
the tension was palpable and pervasive. A massive military presence was required to contain it.

It would be presumptuous for an outsider to dogmatize about
why it had happened. But I was impressed both by a psychologi-
cal explanation offered by Serif Mardin, and a structural one of
Paul Stirling's. Serif observed to me that in the old days, every
Turkish bosom contained two souls, a *macho* and a Sufi. Kemalism
had done its best to destroy the Sufi: it now had to cope with the
macho on his own. Paul Stirling stressed the fact that Kemalism
had initially transformed only the upper layers of society and
political organization, and had left four-fifths of society untouched.
When economic change and migration disrupted this large residue, there was no organizational form ready to receive it. A visit
to a *gecekonde* with Paul as guide and interpreter, and a long and
illuminating conversation with a local patron, made this situation
visible and concrete. The patron had retained his links with his
natal village, but carved out a fine position for himself in the
town. This position inevitably depended on a double capacity –
to link up with a higher supportive patronage network, and an
ability to control his local clientele. He gave the impression of
being a man of great political skill and moderation, and one who
would not employ violence unnecessarily: but when necessary,
he would have resolution and willingness to use it.

I was also struck by the fact that the next generation of intellectuals no longer upheld Kemalism in the *ulama* spirit. On the
contrary, they had internalized it in a far laxer and more pliable

version. The first generation had known and absorbed Islam proper, and presumably had to struggle with it in their own hearts, or at least to guard against it. They possessed no other spiritual equipment, and had to use it and turn it against itself. They had fought the inner fight with the help of the only weapon they possessed – a fundamentalist, rigid, uncompromising, scholastic cast of mind.

Members of the next moral cohort, on the other hand, when reflecting on the endemic conflict between the modern faith and the folk tradition, were more eager to seek a compromise, and thus escape the festering tension. They were psychically able to do so. The underlying argument is present in an article of Nur Yalman's.[3] It runs, roughly, as follows: Kemalist secularism had been inspired by an exclusive acquaintance with, and repudiation of, the uncompromising High Islam of the central religious establishment, and the assumption that this *was* Islam. No doubt it was desirable to repudiate that form. But it is a mistake to equate it with *all* Islam. It is only one special version of it. Ought we not to look at the more humane, earthly or earthy, though less orthodox, Islam of the Anatolian villages? Let us look to the people. May we not find there a more flexible and open faith, and a set of values compatible with the new secular aspirations, closer to the real folk traditions, and perhaps capable of giving the new society valuable support? Serif Mardin's work on a semi-modern, semi-Sufi Anatolian revivalist movement, in effect takes this argument a step further: is there not a great potential for both internal and external harmony, for adaptation to the new world, in the indigenous, *and* endogenous, spiritual strivings of popular Islam and its spiritual leaders?

If there is something in such a quest, a new synthesis could perhaps emerge which would satisfy both needs. On Serif Mardin's account, an example might be the Nurci movement, with its roots in Anatolian folk mysticism, but elaborated by a

[3] Nur Yalman, 'Islamic reform and the mystic tradition in Eastern Turkey' in *European Journal of Sociology*, vol. 10, 1969, no. 1, p. 41. See also Serif Mardin: *Religion and Social Change in Modern Turkey: the case of Bediüzman Said Nursi*. Albany: SUNY, 1989.

thinker conscious of the challenge of modernity, and eager to incorporate its lessons. David Shankland's as yet largely unpublished work on the Anatolian Alevi and their links to Kemalism lends further support to this theme. Once upon a time, Russians vacillating between populism and Marxism asked anxiously whether perhaps Russia could bypass capitalism, and proceed straight from the village commune to socialism. Similarly, this intellectual trend seems to express the aspiration to proceed straight from the rural shrine to a relaxed, modern, enlightened religiosity, bypassing the stage of puritan scripturalist fundamentalism, to which the Iranian and much of the Arab worlds now seem to be committed. If this were to happen, the Turkish way to ideological modernity would indeed be original. There is also the fact that in a way, Turkey is a mirror-image of the 'small nations' of Eastern Europe. In *their* case, peasants sharing, more or less, the same culture, had to become a nation by acquiring their own *High* Culture, state and elite. In Turkey, a pre-existing military-administrative elite, well habituated to having and running its own state, had to acquire its own folk base, and almost contingently alighted on the Anatolian peasantry. Thereby it took that peasantry, not altogether willingly, into the European zone where modernity is nationalist, rather than the Middle East where it went fundamentalist.

But perhaps it will all turn out to be much more prosaic. Recent researches by Richard and Nancy Tapper in a prosperous small West-Anatolian town makes one wonder about the possible emergence of a Middle Turkey, on the analogy of Middle America, where respectability and normality find their expression in an unselfconscious blend of Kemalist republicanism and urban Islam, fusing Turkish and Muslim identity in an apparently seamless web of symbol and sentiment, as Ottoman and Islamic identity had once been fused. Being a good citizen and a Muslim may blend once again.[4]

---

[4]   Nancy Tapper and Richard Tapper, 'The birth of the Prophet: Ritual and gender in Turkish Islam', *Man*, vol. 22, no. 1, March 1987, and 'Thank God we are secular!: Aspects of fundamentalism in a Turkish town' in L. Caplan (ed.), *Studies in Religious Fundamentalism*, London, 1987.

The Ottoman empire had been exceptional in the Muslim world in that it escaped, at any rate in its central areas and after its early period, those two conspicuous features of the world of Ibn Khaldun – the tribal base of the polity, and the fragility of the state. Here there was an individually, and not tribally, collectively recruited elite, and this was combined with a highly developed version of the millet system. A mamluk-type ruling class was superimposed on a set of self-administering but coercively weak religious communities. The two features were presumably connected: the millet system was most conspicuous in the effectively governed parts of the empire, and much less so in the marginal periphery, where the world of Ibn Khaldun survived.

The Turkish way to modernity seems to be similarly distinctive. The modernizing ideology concentrated on secularism and the state, and was relatively free of rigid commitments to economic or social doctrine. The successors of the *timar*-holders admittedly did less well, economically, than the latter-day samurai. Could this be because a hereditary feudal class has a better sense of economic management than a category of temporary, revocable, centrally appointed prebend-holders?[5]

The Turkish way to modernity also avoided an emphatically ethnic nationalism when, but for the Enver Pasha adventure, it turned its back on pan-Turanianism. These features have turned out to be a great advantage in comparison with, for instance, societies which modernized in the name of Marxism (not to mention those whose re-affirmation is done in the name of Muslim fundamentalism). The formal ideology of Marxism – contrary to its popular image – is absurdly over-liberal, and in effect anarchist, in its long-term view of the polity and the economy. It envisages both a self-regulating economy and an actually *disappearing* state, thus bizarrely going far beyond the claims of the *laissez-faire* doctrine of the liberals. The liberals want a minimal state, the Marxists commend and anticipate, in theory, its total

---

[5]   See for instance L. Metin Kunt, *The Sultan's Servants,* New York, 1983, or Huri Islamoglu-Inan, *The Ottoman Empire and the World-Economy,* Cambridge, Paris, 1987.

absence. The brutal and sombre Marxist view of political life applies only to class-endowed society and the relatively short run, and is not meant to apply to the order which is yet to come.

It is only in its praxis that Marxism becomes authoritarian: the realities of both economic development, and of running an advanced industrial society, turn out to be incompatible with such over-liberal aspirations. So it is concrete pressures and perhaps local traditions, rather than doctrine, which impel Marxist societies to an extreme, stifling and inefficient centralism. When this centralism turns out to be a constricting incubus, no conceptual tools are available for coping with it. So the problem is severely aggravated by the lack of any system of ideas, *within* the doctrine, which could handle it. As these problems are not theoretically supposed to arise at all, there is no language, internal to the ideology, which could articulate them. The ideologists of the movement were then obliged to cheat in order to inject such notions into their discussion at all. This is of course precisely what they are trying to do at present throughout the socialist world. Kemalism, thanks to its relative doctrinal thinness, is fortunate in not facing such a problem. Its entrenched clauses – political secularism and constitutionalism – are salutary, but not excessively specific. On other issues, it is not exactly inspired, but then, it is not muzzled either. It is capable of pragmatic development, without having to strain at some doctrinal leash.

It is thus that I would relate the Turkish experience to what have been my persistent theoretical concerns. I can only acknowledge and apologize for the inexpert and unprofessional nature of these reflections.

8

Enlightenment Against Faith

Two great things happened in the twentieth century. Physical nature yielded up a very major part of her secrets. It also became clearly manifest, contrary to the erstwhile vibrant faith of many, that the social world had *not* yielded up anything of the kind.

Physical nature is now our humble and despised slave: we have almost nothing to fear from her, though we have everything to fear from the effects of our own socially uncontrolled and per-haps uncontrollable manipulation of her. But when it comes to our understanding of the laws of social development, there has been little if any progress. On the contrary, we have witnessed a total collapse of the most elaborate, best-orchestrated theory of society, born in the nineteenth century – a theory which had also become the state religion, and the object of partial or total belief, for an enormous section of mankind.

The dramatic demise of Marxism is perhaps almost as great an event as the triumph of physics. Hence the life of Andrei Sakharov is probably *the* life of the age: he was profoundly and intimately involved in both of these great events. He had lived the triumph of physics *and* the catastrophe of Marxism. He more than any other one man had helped to end the nuclear monopoly, and thus establish the balance of power – or terror – which is the basic strategic fact of the second half of the century. He helped to forge the means of destruction which govern the distribution of power in our world. It was also he, more perhaps than any other single man (two men at most can rival him), who helped break the internal ideological status quo of his own society. Thus he also contributed to the dismantling of the *intellectual* balance of power, which had for so long defined the world we inhabit.

What kind of man was he, and how did he come to do what he did? The man who emerges from these memoirs is an exceedingly attractive one. If Russians are to be divided into Apollonian and Dionysiac varieties, into the Turgenevs and Chekhovs on the one hand, and the Dostoevskis and Tolstoys on the other, there can be no shadow of doubt as to where he belongs. Given his fate, the astonishing thing is how relatively little turbulence, anguish, doubt and resentment entered his mind, notwithstanding the terrible treatment he eventually had to endure – and how much there was of moderation, optimism, confidence and harmony.

His basic alignment on the question which has haunted Russians comes out very early in the book, when he recollects being taken to church as a boy. He recalls

> the radiant mood of my mother and grandmother returning from church after taking communion. But neither can I forget the filthy rags of the professional church beggars, the half-crazed old women, the oppressiveness, the whole atmosphere of Byzantium, of Russia before Peter the Great – and my imagination recoils in horror at seeing the barbarism, lies and hypocrisy of the past carried into our own time.

The Byzantium which is so passionately and unambiguously repudiated is a code word for something far broader than merely a liturgical style. The next paragraph goes on to qualify this outburst, and stress that there is much to admire among 'those who are sincerely religious' in any faith: some of his best friends are religious, as you might say. But he has no need to say that good people are also found among those who favour the Enlightenment. His alignment, his repudiation of pre-Petrine Russia, is obvious. The contrast with his great opposite number, who loves pre-Petrine and not post-Petrine Russia, and who opposes

Bolshevism not because it differs from the West, but because it is Western, could hardly be clearer.

Sakharov's father was also a physicist and a successful writer of books popularizing physics and, just as significantly, propounded and practised values later perpetuated by the son:

> Father had a favourite saying which expressed his understanding of harmony and wisdom: 'A sense of moderation is the greatest gift of the gods.' He applied this . . . to all aspects of life . . . he approved of an orderly, systematic approach . . . to politics – he would say that what the Bolsheviks lacked most of all was balance.

Sakharov goes on to say that these views had an enormous effect on him, but that an inner ferment and conflict made moderation 'something I could achieve only with great effort'. The overall impression left by the book is not merely that this effort has been successful: but that the inner obstacles had not been quite as formidable as he himself would have it. He teases one somewhat by stressing his 'dislike for self-flagellation and soul-searching': the book, he says, is a 'memoir, not a confession'. This insinuates that much inner torment is left out.

On the internal evidence of the book, my guess would be – and this in no way diminishes his achievement, rather the contrary – that, notwithstanding the astonishing transformations which he had to undergo, these were inspired more by inner confidence and continuity than by inner crisis. The boy repelled by the smell of pre-Petrine Russia was the father of the man who eventually rebelled against the Stalinist and Brezhnevite Byzantium, and he reached his later position without an inner cataclysm. If this serenity is but a mask – and I expect the question will be much discussed – it is, to me, a very convincing one. There is a kind of double bluff – *not*, I hasten to add, any deliberate disingenuousness. Paraphrasing Groucho Marx, my inclination is to say – Sakharov *appears* to be serene, but don't be deceived! He *is* serene.

At the age of ten, he was physically intimidated by a group of boys and an adult into giving information about another boy, who was then murdered (though of course he did not know this would happen, and the murder would in all probability have taken place anyway). He observes that the episode continued to weigh on him. What is significant is that structurally rather similar episodes were repeated much later, with but one difference – the gang of boys were then the KGB. On at least two occasions, hunted men approached him for help, which he was unable to give, and they were murdered soon afterwards, possibly *because* they sought his aid, or so as to intimidate him.

If there was indeed an underlying continuity and stability in Sakharov, this point must not be interpreted in an exaggerated and over-literal sense: he was not born a dissident, not perhaps a born dissident. It wasn't quite that simple, nor quite *that* continuous and smooth. The basic tenor of his soul is that of a man at peace with himself and with the world – *even when the world does not deserve it*. Whether this is a strength or a weakness is a difficult question. It enabled him to achieve what he did achieve, and his achievement is enormous. It may also mean that though he will be counted amongst the most effective reformers of a world which desperately needed reform, he will not be classed amongst its most profound analysts. It took a complex and prolonged development to turn him into an open critic of that world, but, despite truly appalling harassment (notably during the Gorky exile period), he never became wholly alienated from it, and never came to loathe it in his heart. The moderation never deserted him – except, perhaps, when his persecutors tried to unnerve him by insulting his wife.

> I grew up in an era marked by tragedy, cruelty and terror, but it was more complicated than that. Many elements interacted to produce an extraordinary atmosphere: the persisting revolutionary elan, hope for the future, fanaticism, all-pervasive propaganda, enormous social and psychological changes . . .

Initially, when it was at its worst, the terror actually confirmed rather than undermined belief: it was a kind of testimony in blood to the great changes that were taking place.

> Hardly a family remained untouched, and ours was no exception
> . . . Was our family's chronicle of tragedies exceptional? Every family
> I know suffered casualties, and many lost more members than
> ours did.

But he goes on to say that he did not know whether his parents
harboured thoughts on these matters, and that he was content
to absorb communist ideology without questioning it. As for
nationalism, he recalls the early period when the term 'Russia'
had an almost indecent ring, suggesting nostalgia for the pre-
revolutionary period – and also the revival of the cult of national
pride in the thirties.

> But there was nothing chauvinistic about my family's attitude to
> Russian culture, and I do not recall a single derogatory remark
> about other nationalities – rather, the contrary.
>   Now, it no longer seems impossible that the state might openly
> endorse an ideology of Russian nationalism . . . at the same time,
> Russian nationalism is becoming more intolerant, in dissident circles
> as well. This only serves to confirm a viewpoint whose origin lies
> in my youth.

His attitude to Marxism was, I believe, characteristic of that of
many of his generation: speaking of his student years, he notes
that it never entered his head to question Marxism as the ideology best suited to liberate mankind, whilst at the same time he
was left cold, if not repelled, by its specific features – Engels'
outdated Lamarckism, the primitive use of mathematical formu-
lae by Marx, the superficiality of Lenin's work on the theory of
knowledge, and the jargon . . . He adds one further, powerful
and original criticism of his own: he has no use for books which
can be used as doorsteps.

The mixture of overall acceptance of the claims of official
Marxism, with an indifference to not only its theological conno-
tations, but even its salient doctrines (though he does say that
the materialism is 'reasonable enough'), is typical of his time. It
is also significant. There are dissidents, e.g. Djilas, or Wittfogel,

whose disenchantment with Marxism takes the form of finding non-Marxist answers to Marxist questions. This is not at all the case, for better or worse, with Sakharov: Marxism in the end simply passes him by, with its doorstep-thick scholasticism ('19th century German pedantry' is his own phrase), infantile mathematics and all. Sakharov's development never takes the form of an inner dialogue with Marxism. When he emerges from the darkness of credulity, he enters, almost untroubled, into that sunshine of Enlightenment (had he ever left it?) where common sense, science and basic human decency constitute adequate guides. There is, for better or for worse, no real social counter-theory. This also is perhaps of the essence of that *perestroika* which he helped lead: it is to be a pragmatic compromise, rather than a coherent Reformation.

This inner serenity also differentiates him from others who were deeply scarred by the Soviet experience – for instance, his friend Valentin Turchin, now settled in America, whose remarkable *Inertia of Fear* and *The Scientific Worldview* (Columbia University Press, 1981) describe a truly Cartesian experience: if one's entire social environment is made up of a tissue of falsehood, if circular reasoning and coercion jointly combine to constitute a real Malignant Demon, how can one ever escape his clutches and emerge into truth? How can one ever attain confidence and certainty? One would assume this to be a common experience of anyone who lost his faith in the USSR: but in Sakharov's case, either science, or the illumination of that post-Petrine, but pre-Bolshevik Russia, to which he gives his loyalty, provides a solid foundation underfoot. Similarly, the outer scars – and they were many – do not really penetrate his soul. There are other dissidents – Amalrik, Zinoviev – who convey the impression that they feel permanently and deeply soiled by the all-pervading mendacity of the Stalin/Brezhnev Byzantium, by its appalling ubiquity and intrusiveness. They feel not only indignant, but also somehow contaminated by the filth. In consequence, they find it hard or impossible to speak of the system without sarcasm, with a kind of grimace touched by self-hate. All this is absent from Sakharov.

Sakharov's persistent and evidently unimpaired moderation and tendency to see (and sympathize) with both sides of an issue, constantly comes out. For instance, after describing his acceptance by a physics research institute and the commencement of his work, he comments on the philosophical status of modern physics, with all its counter-intuitive and unconceptualizable (and unvisualizable) processes. He notes the position of the instrumentalists – who hold that 'everything else should be regarded as just "mathematical apparatus" or a system of secondary concepts not open to direct interpretation' – and of those who, like Einstein, seek a more concrete and intuitively acceptable interpretation, and are repelled by 'a God who plays dice'. Sakharov sees merit in both positions. Marxism contains both realist and instrumentalist elements, and considers those questions to be most relevant to its own position, but Sakharov does not deign even to comment on the Marxist view of the matter.

Whether dealing with rival social systems or with rival philosophies of science, Sakharov is open-minded and his inclination is to seek a compromise. No compulsion drives him towards either realism or instrumentalism. It is interesting that this man, clearly capable of moral firmness and resolution, is, on theoretical issues, so very inclined to open-mindedness and doubt. He represents the beau ideal of the Enlightenment: morally firm, yet open in matters of belief. His moral firmness does not need to be fortified by dogmatism. He is altogether free of the fanaticism of his courage, you might say.

He experienced the normal realities of Soviet life. By 1947, Sakharov and his first wife are on the verge of securing a home in central Moscow. This would have greatly eased the problem of going to work at his research institute. In his absence, a KGB man visited his wife and proposed that in return for help with household difficulties, she should covertly report all her husband's meetings. Her refusal to do this was followed, within two days, by expulsion from the new home. They eventually find a room in the Academy of Sciences hotel, which brings him in touch with Sergei Vavilov, eventually President of the Soviet Academy of Sciences – at the very same time as Vavilov's own brother, the biologist Nicolai Vavilov, was perishing in the camps. Sergei Vavilov was obliged to meet Lysenko every week, though it was Lysenko who bore the main responsibility for Vavilov's brother's death. Sakharov reports the story that Sergei was induced to accept the post by the reflection that otherwise it would go to Lysenko himself, with further catastrophic consequences. As Sakharov notes, the paradox of one brother dying of hunger in prison, and the other heaped with honours, was extreme even for that era, and yet in a way also sums it up. In fact, the case is in no way unique: Lev Razgon's remarkable story 'The President's Wife' deals with the very similar fate of Kalinin's wife – and also, incidentally, of Molotov's. The difference was that President Kalinin pathetically pleaded for his wife, whereas Molotov disavowed his.

The options in Sakharov's life were not restricted to choice of loyalty to systems, or the question of a realistic or instrumentalist interpretation of physics. One great issue in Sakharov's life was the choice between pure and applied science. He is never really free of regrets on this score:

> Recalling the summer of 1947, I feel that never before or since have I been so close to the highest level of science – its cutting edge. I am, of course, irked that I did not prove equal to the task (circumstances are no excuse here).

The first invitation to take part in applied nuclear work came in 1946 – accompanied by a promise of good housing and other valuable perks – and Sakharov turned it down: he hadn't left a munitions plant for the frontiers of physics, merely so as to leave them again after so short a time. The offer was repeated in 1947 and, once again, refused. But in 1948, he observes, nobody bothered to ask his consent. The inclusion in a newly founded research set-up solved his housing problem: he and his family secured a room, too small for a dining table (they had to eat off the windowsill), and they shared a kitchen with ten families, and a lavatory with an unspecified larger number, and with no bath or shower. But it *was* in central Moscow. He comments

we were delighted . . . no more noisy hotels or capricious land-
lords . . . so began four of the happiest years in our family life.

Sakharov makes no bones whatever about the happiness which
accompanied his work on the bomb.

> No one asked me whether or not I *wanted* to take part in such
> work. I had no real choice in the matter, but the concentration,
> total absorption, and energy that I brought to the work were my
> own . . . I would like to explain my dedication – not least to myself.
> One reason . . . was . . . the opportunity to do 'superb physics' . . .
> The physics of atomic and nuclear explosions is a genuine theo-
> retician's paradise . . . A thermonuclear reaction – the mysterious
> source of the energy of the sun and stars, the sustenance of life
> on Earth but also the potential instrument of its destruction – was
> within my grasp. It was taking shape at my very desk.

But that was not all there was to it. He was not merely providing
arms for the rulers of the USSR in return for the opportunity to
indulge in superb physics. On the contrary, he assents that he
feels *confident* (my italics) that infatuation with physics was not
his primary motivation. He could, he wryly observes, have found
some other problem in the subject to keep himself amused. On
the contrary: he believed that this work was *essential* (his italics).
He says, in these very words, that he considered himself a soldier
in this new scientific war.

Why was it a just or justifiable war? He mentions the principle
of strategic parity and nuclear deterrence, adding that these principles 'even now seem to some extent to justify intellectually the
creation of thermonuclear weapons and our role in the process'.
(Later, as a dissident, he was to advise *the West* to make sure of
parity: his attraction to the principle of peace through parity
seems deep.) But he goes on to add that his initial zeal, and that
of his colleagues, was inspired more by emotion than by intellect.
He knew of course not only of the 'monstrous destructive force',
but also the price:

the casualties resulting from the neglect of safety standards and the use of forced labour in our mining and manufacturing industries.

Sakharov, a good man (which I hold him to be), was helping to build an appalling weapon for Stalin and Beria to use, whilst familiar, from personal experience, with the nature of their regime, and whilst knowing full well that it was being built with the help of slave labour, and at the cost of the death of many of the labourers; but this knowledge only

> inflamed our sense of drama and inspired us to make a maximum effort so that the sacrifices – which we accepted as inevitable – should not be in vain.

This is one of the central paradoxes of Sakharov's life, and his admirably honest memoirs help one understand it. He is superbly consistent, and goes on to endorse – on balance – the hawks in the West. He expresses sympathy both for Robert Oppenheimer, who wept at his meeting with Truman, *and* for Edward Teller, who faced partial ostracism for his determined advocacy of the development of the H bomb. But all in all, Teller was right, and it was precisely (Sakharov actually spells this out) Teller's experience of communism in Hungary in 1919 which put him on the right lines. Had the West not done what it did

> the Soviet reaction would have been . . . to exploit the adversary's folly at the first opportunity.

Hawks of the world unite, someone might observe with sarcasm at this point.

But there is far more to it than that. Two threads underlie Sakharov's position here, and also provide the clue to his subsequent development. One is, that nuclear deterrence and balance do work; only later, did he come to be imbued by the sense of their precariousness. The other was his transitional belief in a kind of rough symmetry, in moral merit, between the two social systems: subsequently, he also came to be largely but not wholly persuaded of the erroneousness of this fall-back position.

Sakharov notes that his own later fate is strikingly similar to Oppenheimer's, but that in the 1940s and 1950s his position was 'practically a mirror image' of Teller's – 'one had only to substitute "USSR" for "USA" '. An intriguing footnote to history hinges on Sakharov's view that had the USA not developed the H bomb so early, the USSR would not have done so either – not from any reluctance, but simply because early Soviet work was 'the fruit of espionage'. At that stage, had the Americans not possessed something worth stealing, the Soviets would have had no base on which to start.

Sakharov was to remain a denizen of 'the Installation' – 'the secret city where those developing atomic and thermonuclear weapons lived and worked' – for some 20 years, till the revocation of his clearance in 1968. The Installation had interesting labour management problems: long-term prisoners, with nothing to lose, were liable to rebel, and had in fact done so on a previous occasion, and had been ruthlessly repressed. The labour force was then replenished with (relatively) short-term prisoners, who consequently were not inclined to such desperate measures. But that in turn gave rise to a new problem: what was to be done with them when their sentence expired? To release them altogether was out of the question, they might disclose the location of the Installation. A simple and elegant solution was available: exile them to Magadan and similar places where they could tell no tales.

On one occasion, a researcher lost a secret part from a nuclear device, and was arrested. He was fortunate enough to succeed in persuading his interrogators to search the sewer pipes. The KGB cordoned off the area where the sewer pipes emptied into the river, and spent three days chopping through frozen excrement. They found the missing part. The culprit was freed, but sacked. But Sakharov drily observes, as someone endowed with both state secrets and holes in his pockets, he could neither be allowed to leave, nor be employed, nor inform anyone of his plight. Only one exceptionally brave individual dared associate with him. However, he survived, and now writes science fiction for a popular

science magazine, which seems both a fitting and a quite un-
usually happy end to the story. The entire episode conveys the
true flavour of Soviet life.

Sakharov comments:

> We were encouraged to abandon ourselves to our work by the ·
> fierce concentration on a single goal, and perhaps also by the
> proximity of the labour camp and the strict regimentation. We
> saw ourselves at the centre of a colossal enterprise on which co-
> lossal resources were being expended. We shared a general deter-
> mination that the sacrifices made by our country and people should
> not be in vain. *I certainly felt that way myself.* (My italics)

As for 'grand' science, the hope of doing it receded. He had
some idea on which he hoped to work, and mentioned it to a
fellow physicist, who was amused and said – 'so you want to do
real physics and not just be a bombmaker anymore'. Sakharov
adds that it was virtually impossible to combine such basically
incompatible occupations.

Here then is the baseline: a fine scholar working on the production of devastating weapons for a regime whose treatment of
people he knows to be vile, in an institution closely linked to a
concentration camp and using its labour; but he is deeply committed to the enterprise because the sacrifices justify the end, the
attainment of nuclear parity. From this baseline, how did he
reach his later position?

One factor was the fate of a science other than physics. Sakharov
knew that the two crucial sciences were physics and biology, and
Lysenkoism continued to dominate in genetics. Sakharov's exceptionally strong position in the system became evident by 1950,
when a commission visited the Installation to check on personnel, and he was asked what he thought of the chromosome theory
of heredity. Acceptance of Mendelian genetics was, as he observes, considered a sign of disloyalty. Sakharov nevertheless gave
the true answer – that the chromosome theory seemed to him
scientifically correct – and this provoked nothing worse than an
exchange of glances between members of the commission. A less

important man was threatened with dismissal for giving the same reply. Genetics of course became crucial for Sakharov when he came to worry about the effects of nuclear testing.

At the same time, he frequently met Beria, a man who, as he reports elsewhere, used his position to drive around Moscow in his limousine, picking out women whom his henchmen then brought to his appartment for a so to speak *nomenklatura* rape. On one occasion, Beria surprised him by asking *him* whether he had any questions.

> I was absolutely unprepared . . . (but) . . . I asked: 'Why are our new projects moving so slowly? Why do we always lag behind the USA and other countries, why are we losing the technology race?' . . . I don't know what kind of answer I expected. Twenty years later, when Turchin, Medvedev and I posed the same question . . . we answered that insufficient democratic institutions . . . and a lack of intellectual freedom . . . were to blame.

Here is the crux. It was the conclusive defeat in the technological and economic race which persuaded men of good will that change was essential. Had Soviet Marxism been able to continue to persuade them that the sacrifices, however terrible, were worth while, because they would eventually lead to a better life, first for Soviet man and then for all mankind, many of them would have continued to accommodate themselves to the horrors.

So at first, the sacrifices were a kind of sacrament confirming the new order. But by the mid 1950s, Sakharov was worrying about the genetic consequences of nuclear testing. When he expressed these fears to a youthful KGB general whom he respected, the latter expostulated:

> The struggle between the forces of imperialism and communism is a struggle to the death. The future of mankind . . . depends on the outcome . . . the victims don't matter.

With hindsight, writing these memoirs, Sakharov asks himself whether the general was sincere or merely indulging in wide rhetoric, and concludes that it was probably both.

By the time of writing the memoirs, Sakharov considered

> such reasoning . . . wrong in principle. We know too little about
> the laws of history. The future is unpredictable; we are not gods.
> We must all apply ethical standards to every action . . . rather than
> relying on the abstract arithmetic of history.

He had not thought so at first, and it was the loss of faith in the historic plan (accepted in outline, even if spurned or ignored in its details) which propelled him to this mixture of intuitive moralism and justificatory historical agnosticism. This affirmation seen in isolation comes dangerously close to saying we'd better be moral, because we cannot be effective anyway. His real position is more complex, but this is what, with one part of himself, he does say.

Sakharov is admirably candid about his reaction to Stalin's death:

> I too got carried away at the time . . . in a letter to Klara, obvi-
> ously intended for her eyes only, I wrote: 'I am under the influ-
> ence of a great man's death. I am thinking of his humanity.' I
> can't vouch for that last word, but it was something of the sort.
> Very soon I would be blushing every time I recalled these senti-
> ments . . . I can't fully explain it – after all, I knew quite enough
> about the horrible crimes that had been committed – . . . but I
> hadn't put the whole picture together, and in any case, there was
> still a lot I didn't know. Somewhere in the back of my mind the
> idea existed . . . that suffering is inevitable during great historic
> upheavals . . . But above all, I felt myself committed to the goal
> which I assumed was Stalin's as well: after a devastating war, to
> make a country strong enough to ensure peace . . . In the face of
> all I had seen, I still believed that the Soviet state represented a
> breakthrough to the future.

In due course, he was to lose this faith. Initially, he replaced it by what he himself calls the 'theory of symmetry':

> I . . . came to regard our country as one much like any other . . . all
> nations are oppressed.

In fact, symmetry does not obtain, in politics any more than it does in physics; but he cannot disavow it altogether.

> I came to realise that the symmetry theory needed refinement . . . our regime resembles a cancer cell. And yet I do not mean to be quite so categorical in my assessment as it may sound. I finally rejected the theory of symmetry, but it does contain a measure (a large one) of truth. The truth is never simple.

By the mid 1950s, as he becomes outstandingly successful as a bomb-maker, he also begins to worry seriously about the genetic effect of the testing. This impels him into the public arena by two distinct paths: his calculations concerning the consequences of testing lead him to feel bitterness about the continued power of Lysenkoites, and he becomes involved in the struggle for the suspension of tests.

Krushchev (whom on balance Sakharov assesses positively) authorizes the publication of Sakharov's article about the control of testing: and he also suspends testing, though this turns out to be for seven months only, in the light of what was in Sakharov's view, an unjustified lack of Western response. He takes great pride in his contribution to the 1963 Moscow treaty, which limited atmospheric and some other forms of testing; and by 1964, he also successfully helps oppose the election of a notorious Lysenkoite to full Academician status.

The mid-1960s are crucial: he returns to demanding scientific work ('The principal value of the 1965 paper was its restoration of my confidence in myself as a theoretical physicist'), and also becomes involved in a civil rights case (protests against a sentence of death for a trivial and dubious offence), and in the opposition to the rehabilitation of Stalin. In this connection he goes to see Kolmogorov, the fountainhead of modern probability theory. I am pleased to note that Sakharov has strong doubts about the pedagogic value of the 'new maths' (favoured by Kolmogorov), and observes that

> Euclid served many generations before the advent of Bourbaki.

Sakharov now also came to be influenced by Roy Medvedev (with whom he later broke relations) who, he says, helped him to 'escape from my hermetic world'. Interestingly, he criticizes Medvedev for the very fault which I am inclined to find in Sakharov's own thought:

> I couldn't accept Medvedev's tendency to attribute all the tragic events of the 1920s and the 1930s to the idiosyncrasies of Stalin's personality. Although Medvedev agreed in principle that more fundamental causes were at work, his book failed to explore them. We must still look to the future for a satisfactory analysis of our history.

It is not that Sakharov attributes everything to one man: but there is not too much determined pursuit of those fundamental causes whose absence he deplores in Medvedev's account.

The 1968 Prague Spring is of course another milestone, and he comes to develop his ideas on 'convergence'. Sakharov does not mean by 'convergence' quite what it meant to Western sociologists. To them, it meant a somewhat cynical theory, to the effect that late industrialism and the rule of managers in a consumerist society would produce much the same society everywhere, and hence there may be no need to take too seriously the differences in non-economic institutions and in political climate. Sakharov and his colleagues knew only too well how totally untrue *that* theory is; knew too the non-economic institutions of Soviet power which have held back technological and economic growth, and this failure convinced Sakharov and others, first that this is *not* the future, and second, that even symmetry does not apply after all. What Sakharov does intend is a 'convergence' in a normative sense, as a policy to follow: confrontation should be replaced by co-operation, with meritorious traits of both sides to be incorporated in some general compromise.

The year 1968 also saw his first encounter with Solzhenitsyn, a confrontation no doubt destined to be the object of many studies, and to be treated as another epitome of the split in the Russian soul. Solzhenitsyn, significantly, upbraids him in the very same terms as did the voice of the establishment: 'Any convergence is out of the question'. The man from the establishment had said to Sakharov, 'What you wrote about convergence is utopian nonsense'. The establishment wanted to beat the West in the materialist race, whilst Solzhenitsyn wanted Russia to choose another race altogether: *neither* cared for Sakharov's longing for an alignment with Western fellow-adherents of the Enlightenment. But the Turchin–Medvedev–Sakharov team decided to appeal to the leaders of the Soviet Union for democracy and intellectual freedom in the interests of scientific and economic growth. This, plus 'convergence' in the Sakharovian sense, were of course destined to be the two guiding themes of *perestroika*. Solzhenitsyn criticized this approach for its conciliatory moderation, preferring outright confrontation with the regime. Sakharov notes that what his group wanted was, precisely, a bridge between state and society.

It was in 1970 that Sakharov, now a widower, met Lusia (as he likes to call her) Bonner, who became his second wife in 1972. Her influence on him is of course a matter of evidently intense interest both to the authorities *and* to Solzhenitsyn: the fascinating triangular struggle between Sakharov (post-Petrine Enlightenment Russia), Solzhenitsyn (pre-Petrine Byzantium) and the authorities (pre-Petrine Byzantium clothed in materialist jargon?) is not merely ideological, but also intensely personal, *à la Russe*. In an inter-family row in 1973, Alya Solzhenitsyn lectured the Sakharovs on their excessive concern with the education of their children – other children in the USSR also have no chance of a decent education! Lusia Bonner replied with spirit:

> Don't give me that 'Russian people' shit! You make breakfast for your own children, not for the whole Russian people!

Sakharov comments that Lusia's expostulations about 'the Russian people' must have sounded like blasphemy in that home . . .

Lusia Bonner evidently irritated both the establishment and Solzhenitsyn, and for similar reasons. Both were infuriated by her hold over Sakharov. Her mixed Jewish–Armenian ancestry could hardly be bettered as a red rag to racists in Russia. Solzhenitsyn accuses Sakharov of breaking a moral law, which obliges persons in his position to fight it out and not be concerned with the right of emigration, and for having done so '*in deference to those close to him, to ideas not his own. Such was the inspiration of Sakharov's efforts . . . specifically in support of the right to emigrate, which seemed to take precedence over all other problems*' – a clear allusion to Lusia's alleged influence distorting what, according to Solzhenitsyn, ought to have been Sakharov's priorities. Sakharov comments that there is something demonic about all this, reminiscent of the *Protocols of the Elders of Zion* . . .

Sakharov here also settles his scores with *The Oak and the Calf* (not a pub, but Solzhenitsyn's book about dissidence, from which the above quotation is taken by Sakharov). What he says is clear. After admitting the justice of some of Solzhenitsyn's criticisms of the West, he goes on to say

> The West's lack of unity is the price it pays for the pluralism, freedom, and respect for the individual . . . It makes no sense to sacrifice them for a mechanical, barracks unity . . . Solzhenitsyn's mistrust of the West, of progress in general, of science and democracy, inclines him to romanticise a patriarchal way of life . . . to expect too much from the Russian Orthodox Church. He regards the unspoilt northeast region of our country as a reservoir for the Russian people where they can cleanse themselves of the moral and physical ravages caused by communism, a diabolic force imported from the West . . . If our people and our leaders ever succumb to such notions . . . the results could be tragic.
>
> I differ from Solzhenitsyn on the role of religion in society. For me, religious belief, or the lack of it, is a purely private matter.

Sakharov's first press conference, given on 21 August 1973, was also the one which evoked the greatest response. After that, the scenario accelerates rapidly, and also enters the public domain of the international press: hunger strikes, the Nobel prize, Carter hearings, much harassment by the KGB including theft of manuscripts (e.g. early versions of these memoirs), probably KGB-induced convulsions of a grandson, trips abroad by Lusia for medical treatment, more involvement in civil rights cases, also more theoretical physics, and finally the Afghanistan war and opposition to it.

The climax is exile to Gorky with the extreme and sustained and horrible harassment. The KGB was no longer able to kill, or at any rate, did not kill Sakharov. It was, however, either instructed, or permitted, to harass him and his family, and emerges as a bizarre bunch of playful tricksters with a penchant for murderous horseplay. The logic of the situation is not fully clear: it was no longer possible to silence Sakharov effectively, but the authorities could not tolerate his presence in Moscow, and so compromised by making his life hell in Gorky – and yet did not effectively prevent communication between him and the outside world. They would seem to have made the worst of both worlds, but perhaps they calculated (rightly) that they could thereby discourage intra-USSR support for him. The shift of Sakharov's concern, from the general issues of arms restraint and liberalization, to individual civil rights cases, continued, and for this he was denounced by some fellow-dissidents and Solzhenitsyn, as well as by the authorities, and this her enemies attribute to Lusia. The attempts by the authorities to vilify her reach a high peak in 1976 and 1977.

There can be no doubt about the intensity of Sakharov's love for Lusia – or of his love of science and physics. During the Gorky exile, he also returned to fundamental science and cosmology. One particular speculation which he describes as too fanciful for a scientific paper (no doubt rightly), but which he nevertheless deems worthy of inclusion in these memoirs, runs as follows: suppose that the expansion of the universe is followed at a certain stage by a re-contraction, terminating in that superdense condition which had preceded the primal Big Bang. If so, we are left with a series of universes such that the end of one also constitutes the commencement of the next. Is it conceivable that, during the exceedingly long span granted to each such universe, intelligence develops to such a high point that it is capable of devising a method for the transmission of information from one universe to the next, by means of a code which somehow survives the super-condensed stage – somewhat, I suppose, as the black box in an aeroplane is meant to survive its crash and preserve valuable information, though of course the means deployed would have to be immeasurably more sophisticated.

The speculation is indeed wild, but it strikes me as significant: it occurs rather close to a passage in which Sakharov also describes the rhythm of his and Lusia's life during the painful Gorky exile. Every six weeks or so Lusia was able to go to Moscow, for about ten to fifteen days. This also meant contact with the outer world and thus a continuation of the struggle. She would leave food for him in the fridge. Clearly he thought of life without her as a kind of limbo, which he had to live through in order to reach the next cycle of real life in her presence. Yet the limbo was worth it, for it also made transmission of information possible from and to the closed Gorky world. The cosmological speculation about inter-communicating universes, speaking to each other in not merely trans-cultural, but trans-universal codes, across the utter darkness of unimaginably compressed matter, may or may not have any merit: but was it not, for Sakharov, a parable on his Gorky situation?

The exile is finally terminated by Mikhail Sergeievich Gorbachev as a kind of *deus ex machina*, and the new chapter of *perestroika*, in which Sakharov was destined to play such a great part, was about to begin. The book itself, alas, ends at this point.

What do the memoirs amount to? I doubt whether any other single book can convey so vividly, so many-sidedly, and (I believe) so accurately, the realities and options of Soviet life and sensibility over the past half century. Sakharov's life and experiences spanned many of the crucial segments of Soviet life: admittedly he was privileged at certain times, but, contrary to Solzhenitsyn's accusation, he also knew the ordinary Soviet squalor, and the full force of harassment. Morally, he had spanned almost the entire spectrum, from a typical acceptance, characteristic of the period when the system still believed in itself, and transmitted that faith to the very people whom it oppressed and frequently murdered, to the critical but reformist and moderate dissidence, characteristic of one important strand within *perestroika*. His span does not reach out further to those who reject Ivanburg totally and with uncontrollable spasms of disgust, and hold it to be beyond the reach of rational reform, and who seem to relish their pessimism; nor does it embrace the position of those who would change the system, but in a romantic–mystical, anti-rational and anti-Western direction. So what did he stand for, whom did he represent?

I think he answers this when he quotes with approval, early in the book, the following characterization of the Russian intelligentsia:

> In late 19th century Russia there existed something of fundamental importance – a solid, middle class, professional intelligentsia which possessed firm principles based on spiritual values. That milieu produced committed revolutionaries, poets, and engineers.

The point about that class is that it not merely survived, but numerically expanded during the period of Soviet power. No doubt much of it also gave the regime the kind of support which Sakharov himself had initially bestowed on it. Its numbers were swelled by universal education, and by the expansion of the number of jobs which could only be filled by educated people. The values of members of this class resemble those of Sakharov, even if few men can compare with him in stature.

It was always obvious to me, long before *perestroika*, that for every heroic dissident, there was a large number of people who inwardly shared and endorsed the values which inspired dissidence, even if they lacked the desperation, or heroism, or privileged position, which made open dissidence a possible option. The eventual succession of, first disclosures about Stalinism, then the sense of the squalor of Brezhnevism, and finally the full impact of economic–technological failure and backwardness, by their cumulative impact weaned this class from its loyalty to the regime. (It was Brezhnev not Stalin who destroyed Marxism: terror would be and was conceptually accommodated, permanent squalid inefficiency could not.) I had always expected that some measure of liberalization would come in the Soviet Union from the slow increase and thrust of this class, slowly moving like an irresistible sand dune. What I did not foresee (nor I think did anyone else) was that through Gorbachev, quantity would be transmuted into quality: the insidious quiet collective drift of this intelligentsia would become a landslide, and cause a dramatic transformation of the entire moral climate of the Soviet Union.

This has however also meant that the entire structure is now in grave peril. If it collapses, the kind of gradualism which Sakharov favoured would no longer be possible. Those who helped to erode the first secular *ancien régime* by Reason, will then no longer be its heirs. But so far at least, the class and spirit which Sakharov represented, has become, for once, rather weighty, and it may exercise decisive influence. It is now more numerous, perhaps more confident, and has the authority of its technical competence; its tone may find an echo in a partially embourge-oised and educated narod and perhaps it also appeals to those who are frightened by the more extreme alternatives, and who have something to lose. Whether in fact this class now really accedes to power, and will be in a position to implement the spirit which Sakharov exemplified, his deep respect for science *and* a genuine capacity for open-minded doubt, remains to be seen.

9

The Price of Velvet
Tomas Masaryk and Václav Havel

There are some marked similarities between Masaryk and Havel,* and also some significant differences. Both are 'President–Liberators', who helped bring about, or at any rate, give form to, the transition from a repudiated regime, to one more liberal and in due course endorsed by the nation. Masaryk actually found himself being formally attributed this title: somehow, I have the feeling that this precedent will not be followed in the case of Havel. Both were/are intellectuals and moralists, deeply concerned with the moral basis of politics, and in particular, the moral basis of their own participation in politics. Each had, in the days which preceded victory, been part of a small minority of opposition to the regime which they eventually replaced.

Havel opposed a regime which was vile, and outstandingly repulsive even by the exacting standards, in these matters, of 'really existing socialism'; Masaryk, by contrast, opposed a regime whose condemnation remains profoundly contentious, and which he himself only came to reject *very* late in life, and under the impact of rather exceptional circumstances, and after prolonged inner hesitation. Havel's great moral achievement was to defy the

---

* This chapter is based on a review of Václav Havel's (1992) *Summer Meditations on Politics, Morality and Civility in a Time of Transition*. Translated by Paul Wilson. Faber & Faber, London.

revolting communist regime at all and to show that someone at least had the moral fibre to do so; Masaryk's achievement, prior to his fateful decision early in the course of the First World War, was not to defy the regime – he was an active participant in it as Member of Parliament and in other ways – but to fight moral but unpopular causes which often infuriated his compatriots more than the regime. He took a firm stand in support of the unmasking of fraudulent manuscripts intended to demonstrate Czech medieval glories, and he took a firm stand in a ritual murder accusation against a Jew, notwithstanding the fact that in his inner feelings, as he later confessed to Karel Čapek, he never overcame instinctive negative reaction to Jews. To infuriate both the national vainglory and the anti-Semitism of his co-nationals – what a strange way to political fame, or notoriety, for a man who finally made his mark on the world scene as a great *nationalist* leader! But there is logic in this paradox: his nationalism was only justified, as he came to explain in his writings, because the implementation of its programme was at the same time the implementation of an inherently moral historical plan.

In each case – and this is very significant – the transition from the repudiated *ancien régime*, to the more democratic new order, had a *velvet* quality. The complicity in the course of transition with the previous, disavowed regime, has profound implications for the nature of the moral problems faced by the respective Master of Ceremonies, so to speak, of each of the Transitions. This is quite specially true in Havel's case.

The original declaration of the Czechoslovak state in Prague on 28 October 1918, has a profound, historic–philosophic meaning for Masaryk, which he expounded in a whole series of works: it terminated the links between the Czech nation and the Habsburg dynasty, which in turn stood for theocratic absolutism and the Counter-Reformation. Political absolutism, Masaryk was to say contemptuously, was derivative from Church absolutism: 'the theory of the monarch's and state absolutism is nothing but kibitzing of the theoreticians of clerical absolutism and dictatorship' (!) as he says on p. 573 of *Světová Revoluce* (Prague, 1925). The absolutists of the state, whilst eager to liberate themselves

from Church tutelage, were at the same time most eager to inherit some of its infallibility. In this work, incidentally, he also
stressed, very early, the manner in which the infallibility of Bolshevism and that of the Counter-Reformation lead, by an identical path, to the Inquisition. His early rejection of Leninism – in
this he resembled Russell – was based precisely on the fact that
he saw, in its appalling proclivity to Infallibility doctrines and
feelings, precisely those traits which he rejected (even in their
attenuated, age-softened form) in the regime he eventually overturned. One should add that Masaryk's appreciation of Bolshevik
realities was based on an intimate, deeply affectionate, but illusion-
free knowledge of Russia. But the main point is the *meaning* of
the first Czech revolution of this century for its acknowledged
leader (who was, after all, a professional philosopher and a professor). What did it mean to him, why did it fit in with the wider
meaning of history?

What the event in the end meant to him is clear. It has a double
meaning, though the two themes are related, and they confirm
each other. On the one hand, the establishment of the Czech
state is not an isolated event: there is absolutely nothing Sinn
Fein-ish, of 'ourselves alone', of a proud national self-sufficiency,
about Masaryk's thought; there is no question of going it alone,
either ideologically or in political action. Quite the contrary: the
Czech revolution is both vindicated, and incidentally, made feasible, by the fact that it is a part and an example of a much wider
and global process, a replacement of theocracy and absolutism
by democracy, which incidentally carried with it the independence or self-determination of nations. There is not the slightest
element of defiant affirmation of the will of one nation: national
independence is both validated and made possible by being part
of a much wider, and *deeply moral*, process. There is a kind of
other-directedness about Masaryk's thought which is characteristic of the modern Czech spirit, or was until recently, and which
inspired both Masaryk's philosophy and his political strategy.
The political aim had to be vindicated as a corollary of the
overall historical trend, and the strategy consisted above all of
doing things which would persuade the leaders of world opinion

that Czechs were worthy members of the world-historical club. He was a little inclined to confuse the acceptance of the Czechs by History, with their acceptance by the Great and the Good in the West: consequently, he confused national policy with national image-creation and propaganda, and encouraged, unwittingly, the illusion that if this enterprise was successful, the nation would be safe. To believe or presuppose all this was to overrate the firmness, and dedication to the Democratic Direction of History, amongst Western leaders. No wonder that Munich was a trauma for the nation which became, to a considerable extent, Masaryk's reverent disciple.

So, a great deal will depend on whether he did indeed understand that wider process of history correctly: some of his compatriots, early and late, had their doubts on this score, and the debate concerning Masaryk's reading of history is one of the most interesting themes in Czech intellectual life. Incidentally, Masaryk's 1925 book was in due course translated into English as *The Making of a State*, whereas the Czech title means *World Revolution*. The English version can be justified on the grounds that it gives the reader a far more accurate account of the actual contents of the book, which is a fascinating description of Masaryk's activities and thoughts during the First World War period, which eventually led to the establishment of the Republic. A subsidiary reason for the English title is that the Western publishers did not like the Bolshevik-sounding stress on *revolution* in the title. But in a deeper sense, the English title is an appalling mis-translation: the Czechs weren't creating their own state out of some capricious wilfulness or opportunism, they were, on Masaryk's account, doing it because this was part of an overall trend which was both global and deeply moral. Masaryk wanted it clearly understood that he would not be seen indulging in state-creation, unless it was manifest that it was morally right to do so *and* history had decreed that it should be done – and these two conditions were linked to each other, for history did not do things lightly or without good cause. Like the men who drafted the American Declaration of Independence, he was not going to indulge in state-creation lightly, without due cause and deep philosophic reflection. No State Formation without Philosophic Justification! The victory of their nationalism was the victory of democracy, reason, sobriety, scepticism, individualism. It was not something to be undertaken lightly.

But, and this is the second theme in Masaryk's interpretation of the great transformation, the Czechs weren't merely jumping onto a bandwagon, belatedly and without having made much of a contribution to it. They had once, in the late Middle Ages and early modern times, been at the very heart and forefront of that movement which they were now re-joining: *that* was the deep meaning of Czech history. The Czech Hussite proto-Reformation of the early fifteenth century was crucial and was followed by the socially radical practice of the Taborites ('Tabor is our programme' was one of Masaryk's mottoes); by the militarily brilliant defence of this movement by Jan Žižka in defiance of the crusading and imperial forces; and a little later, by the elective monarchy of George of Podebrady, with his historically premature scheme for international peace and security. All this showed that the Czechs were not passive beneficiaries, but distinguished contributors to that movement which had at long last prevailed in 1918, and which amongst other things established the Czechoslovak state.

The Czechs had been deprived of this distinguished and pioneering role in the world trend towards democracy by the outcome of the Battle of the White Mountain, and the whole meaning of Masaryk's revolution was precisely the reversal, after 300 years, of the verdict of that battle. Otto von Bismarck was another person who, it appears, once spent an entire night pondering on 'what if' the Battle of the White Mountain (which in 1620 decided the victory of the Counter-Reformation in the Czech lands, and for 300 years excluded the Czechs from the political map of Europe) had only gone the other way: Czech Bohemia would have remained Protestant, it would have aligned itself with Protestant Prussia, Austria would have remained an insignificant Marchland, and Protestant Bohemia would have helped Prussia to dominate the Danube valley and open the way to Baghdad. (To dream of beginning the *Drang nach Osten* in the seventeenth century would seem anachronistic, but let that pass.) Masaryk's opponents, as he himself mentioned (*The Making of a State*, p. 595), invoked Bismarck's one-night reverie in justification of their Catholicism and Austrophilia: what a good job we *did* indeed lose on the White Mountain, for otherwise the Prussians would have Germanized us in the course of using us as their Protestant allies. This is of course the Austro-Slavism argument, clearly articulated in 1848, and much vindicated in the age of Adolf and Josef: without something like a Habsburg Danubian empire, we (and other small nations of Central and south-eastern Europe) are caught between German expansionism and Russian autocracy. Masaryk himself was much worried by the latter, and not insensitive to the force of this argument throughout his earlier years.

But anyway: for Masaryk, the momentous events of October 1918 in due course became, all at once, the fulfilments of history's deepest design, and a long-delayed correction of the 300-years-old distortion of the history of his own nation. All this being so, one would expect at least a little drama and blood, especially in view of the fact that some of those who had striven for the moral trend of history, had been executed for High Treason against the Habsburg monarchy. Not a bit of it. Though the phrase was not yet current, the revolution and transfer of power of 1918 already had a velvet quality. Masaryk stresses the calm, bloodless character of this *coup d'état* (*převrat*). He himself distinguishes it from a revolution, and notes it only happened after a revolution in Vienna, and after the collapse of the Austrian front in Italy. Everything was done by negotiation, not by violence. It took a fortnight to complete the process: technical problems, Masaryk observes, made it impossible to proceed faster. The new authorities were first of all recognized by the old ones as *jointly* competent and co-responsible (something to be repeated in the second historic vindication of democracy, by Havel, against a much nastier autocracy). It was surely no accident, Masaryk observes, that the new authorities first of all took over the supply ministry, thereby ensuring themselves the control of the military (*The Making of a State*, p. 475). He notes that otherwise the military constituted a grave danger to the newly proclaimed political order, but with supplies well under control, they could be brought to heel.

In Havel's case, the transition was similarly courteous and so to speak technical. He had helped overturn an exceptionally nasty and totalitarian regime (none of this could with justice be said of the order displaced by Masaryk), but it all seemed to be a matter of request and agreement: '. . . even the Communist president resigned at our request [sic]', he notes with pleasure and a touch of surprise. This revolution did indeed proceed in the idiom of requests and resignations.

Once upon a time, Czechs used to throw the agents of foreign powers out of the window of Prague Castle: the first time round, onto pikes, the second time, onto a soft dungheap; but the third time round, a polite request for resignation is graciously accepted, and incidentally, an Assistant Satrap turns around and becomes the new Prime Minister. He was not thrown out of a window of Hradčany Castle. This time, there would have been no dungheap to soften his landing. It is all part of a tradition.

The interesting thing is that Prague Castle has in this century experienced virtually the entire gamut of possible regimes: Habsburg Counter-Reformation traditionalism, Masarykian liberalism, Hitler, a short interregnum, Stalinism, another interregnum, Brezhnevism, and now Havel. But, every single time, the outgoing powerholders negotiated, haggled a bit if they could, and *signed*. President Hácha signed to Hitler, General Toussaint, commander of the German garrison in May 1945, negotiated his retreat with the Czech National Committee. Even K. H. Frank, the last *Reichs-Protektor*, finding that the Czech negotiators disliked addressing him and preferred the German soldiers, politely resigned so as to aid the negotiations. (This did not however save him from being publicly hanged in Prague about a year later.) Beneš handed over to the communists, Dubček signed to Brezhnev, and Masaryk and Havel both tell us in detail how they indulged in political conveyancing. Havel, for instance, tells us with pride (*Summer Meditations*, p. 23) how even the dropping of the term 'socialist' from the official designation of the country, which in other ex-communist countries was 'dealt with . . . in an hour', was in Prague carried out with parliamentary propriety. Come to think of it, Prague must possess a unique store of experience in Political Conveyancing, and the Law Faculty of Charles University really should institute a special Chair in this discipline. (All this procedural fastidiousness did not at all times prevent a fair amount of murder taking place after some at least of the negotiated transfers of power, notably in May 1945 and after February 1948, but that is another matter.) This is not necessarily a bad thing – why should changes always be hallowed by blood, why should not the partnership of past and present also reach across revolutions? – and maintain the rules of courtesy? – but it may on occasion also raise moral problems. It was not quite the same problem for Masaryk as it is for Havel, but it is interesting to see how they face their respective dilemmas.

Masaryk's problem was that he had to explain why the Habsburg empire, which he had supported for so long, had after all to be destroyed. It could not have been quite so evil, if it had been endorsed for so long. Masaryk, who saw clearly the effects of Counter-Reformation and Bolshevik infallibilism, did not consider the possibility that sanitized, mellowed authoritarianism may be a useful ally of democracy. Many feel nostalgia for it now: better Franz Josef than Josef! Masaryk himself conceded (*The Making of a State*, p. 449) 'after all, we had, almost all of us, for so long maintained and defended the necessity of the Austrian empire to the whole world!' So what had changed now? The Habsburg empire had failed to improve itself, he would say, and so the confrontation of the First World War had to be seen as the struggle between democratic good and authoritarian evil. As one of his most eloquent, and ambivalent, critics, Václav Černý, observes (*T. G. Masaryk in Perspective*, ed. M. Čapek and K. Hrubý, SVU Press, 1981, p. 106), this led him into one or two contradictions. One arose from the somewhat strange inclusion of the Czars in the camp of liberal democracy. The other was far more serious: the overrating of the allegedly unambiguous, and it would seem definitively victorious, democratic revolution, the 'World Revolution' which gave his book its original, Czech title.

This belatedly acquired conviction led to the implicit, but deeply pervasive syllogism, which imbued education in the republic which Masaryk set up. The West is democratic, the West is strong, it is democratic because it is strong and strong because democratic, and because this is the way world history is going. We had been in on this splendid movement sooner than most, as early as the fifteenth century, we had been unjustly deprived of our birth-right, but now we are safely back where we belong, and so we are indeed safe, for the democratic West is very powerful, and all's well with the world. I have had my primary education, and two and a half years of secondary education, in Prague schools, and I can only say that this message emanated, unambiguously and confidently, from the portraits of the President–Liberator which adorned every schoolroom. Major premise: world history is our guide and guarantor. Minor premise: world history has chosen democracy and the West as its agents, and therefore they are irresistible, and their allies (notably ourselves) are safe.

Now what happens to people who very deeply internalize the entire syllogism, notably its major premise, but who are suddenly subjected to a dramatic and traumatic demonstration of the fal-sity of the *minor* premise? Precisely this is what happened to the Czechs in 1938 and 1940. Munich demonstrated that the West was neither firm nor loyal to its democratic acolytes. As Thurber might have said, there is safety neither in numbers nor in demo-cracy nor in anything else. The humiliatingly quick and easy defeat of the French army, previously vaunted as the best in Europe, in 1940, concluded the lesson. But what if the major premise continues to be persuasive, and the historical Trend is still authoritative? But a new minor premise is now available: history appears to be endorsing a new force in the East, capable of defeating the Germans who had defeated the French. The expulsion of three million Germans, fear of German revenge (a fear very vivid after 1945) and recollection of Munich, all jointly propelled any waverers to the same conclusion: there can be no thought of resisting Stalin.

I do not wish to caricature Masaryk. There can be no question of his endorsing democracy simply because he believed it to be strong and victorious. He valued it for quite independent and

moral reasons, but he *also* believed it to be vindicated by manifest historic destiny. And here the trouble is not merely that the
verdict of history is not quite so unambiguous, as his critics insist
(Patočka, Černý, *Masaryk in Perspective*), but, more seriously:
the syllogism which he prepared, and which the educational system
set up under his authority inculcated, led inevitably – given the
replacement of the falsified minor premise by what then seemed
to be the historically correct one – to the passive acceptance of
1948.

The truth is both ironic and bitter, but inescapable: Masaryk's
philosophy of history did eventually lead to 1948. Nothing could
be further from his wishes or values, but the iron laws of logic
lead to this conclusion. If it is *World Revolution* which provides
the signal for the correct political direction in Prague, but if (in
the light of further events) Western democracy turns out to be a
feeble, disloyal and ineffective agent of that great revolutionary
trend, but a more powerful and steady herald appears to the
East . . . well then, the conclusion is easy to draw. Those who
carried out, and those who accepted, the communist coup of
1948, were acting in harmony with the syllogism which Masaryk
had taught them so insistently: they continued to respect the
major premise which affirmed the authority of World History,
they merely replaced the minor premise discredited by Munich
by a new one concerning what now seemed the dominant thrust
of history, and proceeded in accordance with the conclusion.
The *World Revolution* must be implemented in Prague.

Havel's problem, and his solution, are rather different. Havel
does not, like Masaryk, face the awkward question of why he had
turned against a system which he had accepted and endorsed for
so long, and within which he had worked comfortably. Masaryk
openly reports how, early on during the first war, he went to see
the Habsburg viceroy in Prague, a man who was alleged to have
in his possession a list of people due for eventual arrest, which
included Masaryk's own name. '(He) was a decent man, and it
was possible to talk with him fairly openly.' How cosy, how
gemuetlich, personal–political relations were in those days! No,
Havel does not face this problem; the system he opposed was

unambiguously repulsive, and Havel had always opposed it, at considerable cost to himself.

Havel's problem is not why he had turned so late against a system previously held tolerable and worthy and capable of reform, but rather, why, given that the system had been overturned, so much of its heritage was tolerated. Why quite so much velvet? Why try to reassure the old apparat by choosing one of their number for the first free prime minister? Why so much concern with technical continuity of government, somewhat more justifiable in 1918 – the *ancien régime* had the legitimacy of genuine antiquity, and it had no horrifying crimes against humanity on its conscience, whereas the communist one had been guilty of 40 years' sustained mendacity, much murder, sustained blackmail of its own citizens through educational persecution of children; and it was also guilty of high treason and collaboration with a foreign occupation. There are of course good reasons for being soft on the erstwhile collaborators with totalitarianism, and for leaving them with their gains: it is better that they should go and enrich themselves further, rather than smuggle their money abroad; and it is better that they should try to save themselves by conversion to the market, investing in capitalism the funds stolen under communism, than by turning to chauvinism. (One reason for the inevitability of the Czech–Slovak split is that the Czech apparat seems to have chosen the former option, and the Slovak one, the latter – and the two strategies will not mix.) Also, there are too many of those who in one way or another were compromised with the previous regime, too many borderline cases, too many factual ambiguities. There is a plausible theory which maintains that right-wing dictatorships can be liberalized far more easily than left-wing ones, because the old powerholders can be offered the retention of their wealth as their reward for surrendering power, whereas in left-wing totalitarianism there is *only* power, and no wealth, in the technical sense, available for retention. The Czech velvet revolution would seem to provide a counter-example to this: ill-gotten gains, and insider information and positions, are used by the old apparat to turn themselves into the *nouveaux riches*. It may be good for the economy, but all the same, it does leave a bad taste in the mouths of many, including Havel himself.

Havel's own most strongly expressed complaint concerns the moral decline: 'society has freed itself, but in some ways behaves worse than when it was in chains' (*Summer Meditations*, p. 2). There is a great deal that can be questioned, in both parts of this statement. Did *society* free itself? On the very next page, Havel himself remembers that 'a handful of friends and I were able to bang our heads against the wall for years by speaking the truth about Communist totalitarianism while surrounded by an ocean of apathy.' This society had accepted the communist regime, without enthusiasm but with resignation, to such an extent that when liberation came from outer space, those liberated quite literally could not believe their luck, and kept looking over their shoulders nervously for some new set of tanks to arrive to put a stop to it all, though this time there was no place for those tanks to come from.

There is a blatant contradiction between crediting the victory to his society, and also castigating it – correctly, alas – with apathy. And two pages later, once again, he claims victory, not, this time, for society at large, but for his own moralistic style: 'Communism was overthrown by life, by thought, by human dignity' (*Summer Meditations*, p. 5). Was it indeed? Masaryk defended his ultimate political option by a philosophy of history which is interesting, stimulating, contentious, and which turned sour and fatal for the nation politically re-established in its name: but it deserves discussion. Havel's political philosophy – uncompromising decency in the face of sleazy, cynical, opportunist and unscrupulous dictatorship – is heroic and humanly admirable: when, however, it is presented as a *theory* of how such dictatorships can be overcome, or when he goes as far as to say that this was the *only* way to do it (*Summer Meditations*, p. 5), it becomes absurd, indefensible, and can easily be refuted from evidence provided by himself. Two senses can be attributed to Havel's motto *Living in Truth*: it can mean (1) not allowing oneself to be bullied into affirming falsehood by a vicious regime, and (2) not allowing oneself to indulge in high-minded illusions because they make one feel good. Havel's record under (1) is superb. But it would not be altogether easy to give him a clean bill of health under (2).

This contradiction in Havel's thought is taken to task, for instance, by one Peter Fidelius (a pen-name assumed in the days of clandestinity, but which the author chooses to continue to use) in *Literární Noviny*, a Prague literary weekly, of 6 June 1992. Either communism was destroyed by something other than our society, says the author, or our society cannot be quite as rotten as Havel complains: he himself, Fidelius, says he inclines to the latter alternative.

But the first option seems to be endorsed from a surprising source: Petr Pithart, Prime Minister of the Czech lands after the Velvet Revolution, who begins by noting that he had only used this expression in quotation marks: what he means is not that it failed to be velvety, but that there was no revolution. With brutal candour, he says that he refuses to use the term revolution, that there had been no conflict, that the decomposing communist power had only lasted as long as it did because '*we*' had tolerated it, that amongst comparable communist societies we had been the last, and arrived ten minutes after midnight. He proceeds to excoriate the post-velvet authorities (clearly including himself) for culpable light-heartedness and benevolence, notably in being soft on the old power-holders in the Ministry of the Interior. The paper quoting these remarks (*Necensurované Noviny*, no. 12, 1992, a fortnightly) does so with an ironic *No Comment*, as if to say 'listen who's talking . . .'.

Pithart is an erstwhile dissident, and earlier still a communist, who whilst dissident wrote and published, in samizdat and abroad, under the pen-name Sládeček, a remarkable analysis of Czech history and of communist guilt (in which he shared), named simply *'68*. Pithart clearly has a penchant for *mea culpa* self-analysis.

Of the three positions, Havel's, Fidelius' and Pithart's, it is the third which would seem to be correct. Communism was not destroyed by society or by honesty, it could dominate the former and contain or corrupt the latter: it was, whether we like it or not, destroyed by consumerism and Western militarism, plus an outburst of decency and naivety in the Kremlin. Faced by a double defeat in both the consumption and the arms races, the Soviet leadership chose to liberalize politically, in the simple-minded and quickly refuted expectation that this would rapidly lead to an economic improvement. To their credit, a measure of liberalization was to their taste anyway, whilst economic liberalization went against the social grain. In consequence, Eastern Europe, some of which was supine, and some of which would have settled for far less liberty than has now fallen from heaven, is free.

So Masaryk's and Havel's moralisms are not the same, and they do not face the same problem. Masaryk was a bit of a puritan as well as a moralist. He does not merely see the link between Counter-Reformation and Marxist Infallibilism; he also dislikes Catholicism for its transcendentalism, which drives its acolytes into that sexual mysticism so conspicuously present in modernist literature, and which Masaryk heartily disliked. It is Catholics, not Protestants, who are susceptible to this. This view led him into difficulty in the case of D. H. Lawrence, whom he was obliged to declare an exception.

Both Masaryk and Havel are open to the accusation that they take far too seriously the Czech national motto, *Truth Prevails*. It cannot be relied upon to prevail, even in the long run, and as Keynes said, in the long run we are all dead. Masaryk used as his background premise a view of the dominant position of democracy in the contemporary historical process, a view which let down those who put their trust in time, in the days of Hitler and Stalin. To do him justice, Masaryk only seemed to embrace this view wholeheartedly when he had a need to justify his choice in the 1914–18 war: previously he struggled on two fronts, defending concrete social realism against the more extreme romantic historicists. Havel, a superb playwright but an amateur social theorist, puts his trust, not in an overall historical theory, but in the eventual victory of simple decency. In as far as he is saying that decency should be maintained come what may, one can only admire him. When he says that this is politically effective and that there is no other way, one must part company with him. Illusions will not do anyone any good.

What had really prevailed in 1989 was consumerism and the all-European endorsement of a system which satisfies its imperatives, as against one which conspicuously fails to do so, and is oppressive and sleazy into the bargain. Democracy and decency obtained a free ride to victory on the back of the consumerist triumph, and we must be duly and deeply grateful for that, but it is dangerous to delude oneself and suppose that they owed the victory to their inherent political appeal. In an ideal world this would be so, but in the world as it is, it is doubtful. We must of course admire those who had bravely stood up for decency even when it was not victorious but perilous: this is why both Masaryk and Havel deserve our admiration. But it does not mean that we must also accept their general theories concerning why victory was guaranteed. Real loyalty to Masaryk lies in respecting truth, however unpalatable, and not to his specific views on history.

The two men differ considerably in what they have to offer at that point. Masaryk's theory is worked out with academic craftsmanship; it is also contentious, and did, ironically, at a later point, lead the nation in a direction he would have abhorred. Havel's theory is one he only affirms when he formulates his credo, but also shows to be mistaken when he concretely describes what actually happened, or when, in his splendid plays, he lays bare the mechanics of how it happened. Communism was not, alas, overthrown by life, by thought, by human dignity, as he affirms. In his realistic moments, in his literary and descriptive work, Havel knows better. There he describes, with superb irony, precisely how it is that truth does *not* prevail. The society Havel knows and analyses so well, and now also excoriates, accepted communism, without enthusiasm but with resignation. Masaryk's conception of democracy was somewhat Protestant and puritan, and he would I think have been embarrassed by some of the allies it acquired in its second coming (a permissivist pop culture and the Counter-Reformation Church). He would probably have shared some of Havel's disillusion, and deplored some aspects of the contemporary scene which are less unaccept-able to Havel.

Still, there is a link between the two men. Havel is enough of a child of Masaryk's republic to recognize explicitly the principle honoured by the first Czechoslovak state, that only *professors* are fit to be heads of state. When he comes to dream aloud and paint the idyll of the Czechoslovakia which he is trying to build (*Summer Meditations*, p. 102 et seq.), he says, in so many words: 'At the head of the state will be a grey-haired professor with . . . charm.' This is indeed the Masarykian model of presidency. The First Republic only had professorial presidents: non-professors, let alone non-academics, need not apply. Even the potential rival of Beneš for the presidency, who was critical of Masaryk as a historian, was a rival *professor*. Had the timing of the collapse of Marxism been different, Prague would no doubt have had a President–Professor in Jan Patočka, and tradition would have been maintained. But times have changed, or no professor with an appropriate record was available.

So the professor offered us an overall theory of what is happening and should happen, whilst the playwright brilliantly described how what really does happen is manipulated into being, whilst saying something quite different in his declarations of faith. Perhaps we need a combination of the two. The French have Racine to tell them how men *should* be, and Corneille to tell them what they are really like: the Czechs have, in Havel, a person who performs *both* tasks, one as theorist and the other as playwright. But it will be interesting to see whether professors or playwrights make better presidents.

10

Reborn from Below
The Forgotten Beginnings of
the Czech National Revival

Jan Patočka is generally recognized as the most influential Czech philosopher of the post-war period. Late in life, he entered the political arena when he founded Charter 77 in protest against the so-called 'normalization' of Czechoslovakia, i.e. against the establishment of Stalinism-with-a-human-face in the wake of the suppression of the Prague Spring of 1968. He died of a brain haemorrhage fairly soon after a prolonged and zealous police interrogation, and possibly as a consequence of it.

Patočka was a remarkable personality, which, as so often happens in philosophy, cast a spell over his audience irrespective of whether or not he was understood or intelligible. In philosophy, he stood for phenomenology and a devotion to Husserl, whose pupil and disciple he was, and to the Greek classical philosophers. He had a great admiration for the English editors and expositors of the pre-Socratics. The one thing which I understood from his lectures when I attended them in 1945 was that, in his view, something tremendous happened to the human condition with the coming of Greek thought. Apparently, it marked and distinguished for ever those who came under its influence. Much more than that I did not understand, but the intensity of his manner somehow kept me coming to the lectures. His thought and style were convoluted, and when I pointed this out to him and said that his sentences were virtually Germanic in form, he accepted this with pleasure, saying that the Czech language needed something of the kind, if it was to be fit for anything more than just buying and selling. He hoped to make the language less plebeian by making it more convoluted; in philosophy, this meant he made himself obscure, but his thoughts on Czech history are intelligible and exceedingly interesting. He had no aversion to a complex German style and the present work was actually written in German. (The volume contains both the original and a Czech translation, though not one written by himself.)

The circumstances of the composition of the text are interesting. It was originally written in the dark early years of normalization, the early 1970s, in the form of letters addressed to a German woman friend of Patočka's living in the Federal Republic. Somewhat coyly, the editors refrain from disclosing the name of the recipient of these letters. The secret has, however, not been kept, as she is identified in a study of Patočka by Erazim Kohák (*Jan Patočka: Philosophy and selected writings*; reviewed in the TLS of 5 October 1990). The editors also note that no unambiguous answer can be given to the question of whether this is basically a personal text, or whether Patočka contemplated eventual publication. Some personal remarks and stylistic idiosyncrasies suggest the former. A corrected typed version of approximately half the manuscript exists, while the second half exists only in a single version, which, however, is a clean copy. The events of 1968, which constituted the immediate past and the decisive background of the situation in which the work was written, are not mentioned, but it is not unreasonable to suspect that the book is really about them.

Here we have an important thinker explaining his nation's history and character to a woman who (as was suggested to me by a person familiar with the background of the volume) was considering coming to join him in Prague. Here a man is trying to explain a family tragedy, so to speak, and indeed the family weaknesses which had brought it about, to a prospective partner, who may come to live in the family milieu, and, of course, in doing so, he is naturally also trying to explain these things to himself. There can be few nations in Europe (though probably there are some) which live on terms of quite such constant intimacy with their own history as do the Czechs. For Czechs, historicism is virtually a way of life. Patočka quotes the historian of Czech literature, Arne Novák: 'Czech historicism has long stood in the service of the Czech national idea, and it is possible to describe it without exaggeration as one of the most powerful agents of national education.'

The Czechs have no humorous *1620 and All That* (it certainly deserves to be written), which would sum up the folk clichés of Czech history, but in this book we possess, not a derisive, but at any rate a sharp and sometimes exceedingly harsh account by an important thinker of the forging of the historic identity of his nation. Czech history happens twice over: the original story as it actually was, prior to the near disappearance of the nation in the late seventeenth century, at any rate as a fully equipped all-round polity, and the sustained rediscovery, re-interpretation and political use of that same history during the national resurrection which begins somewhere around or shortly before the turn of the nineteenth century.

The first generalization Patočka allows himself is to distinguish the Czechs from all their neighbours, Germans, Austrians, Poles and Magyars: all these, he notes, drew their political class from the upper strata, freed for political tasks. This may have its disadvantages, he adds, for such men may have acted badly, but at least they did act, they were not mere scholars and secretaries (Patočka feels a special contempt for the arch-secretary Beneš). Notwithstanding various social cataclysms, these neighbours remained seigneurial nations right up to the Second World War, taking their values from the lordly class. The Czech fatality was the lack of anything similar, he says, so that Czechs were deeply different from their neighbours in thought and feeling, even when they took over their ideas. Tomáš Masaryk was an exception, but he remained isolated and left no successors. The Czechs, Patočka says, were the first nation to be successfully reborn *from below* (an example to be followed in the Balkans and on the Baltic). For this very reason, the Czechs, not despite but because of their smallness (to be taken in terms of quality not numbers), are of more than local significance: they were (though he does not use these words) pioneers of birth-from-below.

Ironically, but perhaps correctly, Patočka sees the birth of a real modern Czech identity in the Baroque period and in Catholicism (although the nationalism mythology in due course focused on the proto-Protestant Hussites of the early fifteenth century). There was originally 'the hope that the Habsburgs will learn to evaluate correctly the significance of the Czech lands and bring back their seat to Prague . . . the hope that a voluntary counter-reformation, carried out with maximal intensity, will restore the lustre of the Czech name in the eyes of Catholic Europe.'

So the now forgotten first beginnings of the Czech national revival, quite contrary to the later self-image, were not Protestant but Catholic. This led to the creation or invention of the great Czech Catholic saint, John of Nepomuk, based on the conflation of two figures, one of them fictitious (and due to have, though Patočka was not to know this, a new set of major celebrations in the town of Nepomuk this very year). The fictitious one was allegedly martyred, thrown into the Vltava from Charles Bridge at a point which remains marked, for refusing to disclose the secrets of the confessional concerning the Queen's goings on (a respect for the privacy of the life of royal personages which should perhaps endear John of Nepomuk to contemporary England).

Here the plot thickens, and the general pattern emerges. Contrary to its later image, Czech nationalism begins from within Catholicism, and in opposition to the Enlightenment: 'The Czech lands were not merely retarded, they were eccentric in the opposite direction, in a backward movement. When the Enlightenment came in the form of the new Teresan school order . . . with the prospects of social advance only through study in German, Czech-hood carried the opposite principle. It strengthened the resistance to the Enlightenment.' And yet, Patočka goes on to say, this new Czechdom of smallness was also greatly aided by the feared Enlightenment – through Joseph II's emancipation of the peasants. The Czech farmers *were* the Czech nation, and they could now migrate to the towns where they were subject to state justice like anyone else. A linguistic rather than territorial nationalism was born, to which the gentry remained alien. Here begins what Patočka deliberately calls *little* Czechdom – perhaps a good translation would be 'Little Czech-land-ism', on the analogy of little-Englandism. (It is a notion not without some use when trying to understand the first government of the new Czech Republic.) Patočka's polarities are now clear: on the one side, linguistic nationalism, egalitarianism and smallness, and on the other, a territorial state, trans-linguistic patriotism, a sense of noble tasks. History has led the Czech nation into the option he clearly does not favour. The Masarykian vision saw the Czechs as premature Reformers, a thwarted *avant-garde* of progress, eventually restored to its rightful inheritance by the final victory of democracy over medievalism in 1918. Patočka by contrast sees the Czechs as wasting their opportunity, first by aristocratic irresponsibility and then by religious enthusiasm, the two jointly depriving them of a state and condemning them to rebirth from below, the price of which is psychic pettiness.

The theme underlying Patočka's argument is in effect a kind of Anatomy of Smallness – but smallness taken not in a simply quantitative sense. Small is not beautiful – not this kind of smallness, anyway. The outstanding contemporary Czech analyst of historical nationalism, Miroslav Hroch, does something similar, using the terms in a way which makes the Danes into a big nation and the Ukrainians into a small one: what he meant is that the former had a complete society while the latter had to, as it were, belatedly grow their own higher social organs, adding them to a previously incomplete organism. This usage and the vision inspiring it are closely similar to Patočka's. Smallness here becomes a complex notion with a number of constituents: linguistic rather than territorial patriotism, reflecting a fragmented vision devoid either of the erstwhile medieval unity or of its Enlightenment successor/surrogate, in effect turning to what divides men for lack of that which unites them; the building up of a society from below, by a tenacious yet petty struggle for each small advantage – small aims and gains, no great vision, egalitarianism. The Big, by contrast, would be hierarchical (socially complete), committed to an overarching human unity rather than parochialism and identification with contingent linguistic idiosyncrasies, and endowed with vision, capable of producing individuals able to take big, total, decisions and to face serious sacrifices.

The question which Patočka is pursuing, with anguish and bitterness, is the manner in which the historical Cunning of Reason has consigned the Czechs to the wrong option, much to his own regret. He finds some consolation in the reflection that at least we Czechs have pioneered this kind of smallness, have explored its social potential. The first sinners were the medieval Bohemian aristocracy, great *frondeurs*, who irresponsibly thwarted the aspirations of the Přemyslíd and Luxembourg dynasties for strong state-creation (with a touch of an Eastward mission?), eagerly accepted the land-grabbing benefits of religious reformation, but lost interest once they had their hands firmly on the land. Patočka does not altogether share the conventional Czech enthusiasm for Hussites, though he does not deny them greatness. But it was greatness in a questionable cause, and he has his doubts concerning the retrospective inclusion of Jan Hus in a kind of humanist club. He barely hides his distaste for that later avatar of Czech Reform, Petr Chelčický, with his ultra-egalitarianism (rejection of all hierarchy, religious or political, as inherently pagan) and his pacifism. (Like the English extremists later, the Czech zealots proceeded from revolutionary zeal to subsequent pacifism.)

Altogether then, Patočka does not seem too much turned on by the Hussite period. Masaryk was disappointed in it because by the later part of the fifteenth century the aristocracy betrayed the peasantry, increased its own oppressive privileges, and so failed to pursue the initial religious egalitarianism of the Hussites into a modern egalitarianism. As good social democrats, the fifteenth-century Bohemian nobility clearly won't pass muster. Masaryk's critics were not unwilling to point out that his own values were open to the charge of anachronism. The Hussites, as his Catholic opponent, the historian Pekař, would insist, belong to the Middle Ages and the Church, which they emphatically did not wish to leave, and not to the Enlightenment. Patočka, however, can hardly complain that the Hussites were incapable of firm decision or total sacrifice (incapacities which constitute his complaints against the modern Czech), so they do not fail his criteria, which in a way are more timeless than Masaryk's: a cult of heroism is more widespread than liberal democratic secularism. But Patočka does not seem to care too much for their egalitarianism. The egalitarianism of the religious enthusiasts provides a charter, a kind of precedent and justification, some four or five centuries later, for the less heroic egalitarianism of the servants liberated by grace from above, which Patočka so dislikes. He also deplores the failure to build a strong monarchical, un-ethnic and hierarchical Bohemian state, such as he would evidently have preferred, whether the failure springs from aristocratic selfishness or popular religious enthusiasm or the crisis provoked as a reaction to that enthusiasm.

At the turn of the nineteenth century, Patočka notes, the aristocracy and part of the Enlightenment were merely patriotic (i.e. oriented towards the country, rather than towards one of its two languages), while it was the conservatives and the romantics who jointly turned towards a linguistic nationalism, which defines the nation in terms of shared language rather than shared citizenship. Early in the nineteenth century, there was a philosopher priest–professor in Prague, Bolzano, of part-Italian, part-Austrian origin, a great figure now recognized in the West as a precursor of modern philosophy of mathematics and science, and an indirect ancestor of Wittgenstein. But he was also of great importance locally, for he loved theology and mankind as well as mathematics. This other love led him to favour a non-ethnic Bohemian patriotism which would be kind to the then underprivileged Czechs (almost a definition, for those who at that time rose socially became Germanized), *and* a theology which in effect treated true Catholicism as a coded Enlightenment, a tolerant love of humanity rather than a claim to exclusive Revelation. (No wonder that Bolzano had his troubles with the Church authorities.) Patočka elsewhere expressed his regret at the fact that Bohemia failed to follow the Bolzano political option, a regret shared by the late J. P. Stern in his *The Heart of Europe* (1992). But it was not followed.

So the new-style nationalism was born without the benefit of the Enlightenment, whether naked or presented as the true hidden message of Catholicism, as Bolzano would have had it. To be precise, this nationalism was hostile to the intellectual content of the Enlightenment, in which it saw centralization and Germanization (the Enlightenment meant, so to speak, that German replaced Latin as the bureaucratic language), though the institutional reforms which the Enlightenment brought (emancipation of peasants) greatly aided this nationalism by providing it with its opportunity and clientele. This trend was then modified by Slovaks from the kingdom of Hungary, where the Counter-Reformation had failed to penetrate, and they, in conjunction with the historian Palacký, discovered the significance of Hus and his period, and so linked this mood to the earlier non-Catholic strand of the Czech tradition. This then, he says, was the basis on which, slowly, a new nation and society was erected: 'rooted in the people, yet conservative, long devoid of any revolutionary impulse, cautious, feeling its way, devoid of material means and acquiring to a limited extent its spiritual equipment, but tenacious in a peasant spirit and pervaded with the will not to allow itself to be suppressed'.

> Since the Enlightenment, the Czechs are a new nation in the sense that, in contrast to the old, unified, and hierarchical Czech society, relatively indifferent to language, they created a new society of equality, based on the *maternal language*. It was a society of liberated servants. But they did not liberate themselves, that would have called for a revolutionary act. *They were liberated* by a decree of the ruler: they thought in a much less radical manner than did their liberator-ruler. They noted the advantages of liberation, but at heart they were conservative, because the tradition, which linked them to their Czech-dom, was initially antithetical to any kind of enlightenment.

Patočka is hard indeed on his compatriots, in his efforts to understand a certain pettiness of soul. He twice invokes the German

Jewish writer Moritz Hartmann, who in the 1840s published in Leipzig a poem entitled 'Bohemian Elegy', in which he expressed contempt for a nation which is alienated from its own finest action (the Hussite revolt after all?) and which survives by betraying its heritage. Hartmann compares the Czechs unfavourably with the Poles, whose sorrow provokes more compassion than the Czech tragedy of the White Mountain (1620), a kind of Battle of the Boyne in reverse (the Catholics winning), just because the Czechs, at the time, had themselves abjured their pre-1620 past. This, of course, was due to change, and was indeed being changed at the very time Hartmann was publishing his poem. Palacký was rediscovering the Hussites and turning them into the national myth, while at the same time endowing the Habsburg monarchy with a new role and justification, no longer as the champion of the Counter-Reformation, but as protector of small Central European (mainly Slav) nations against German expansionism and Russian autocracy.

The Battle of the White Mountain virtually defines the boundary between the hierarchical open poly-ethnic state of Patočka's nostalgia, and the claustro-philic, egalitarian, small-minded, linguistically defined community which he condemns, and which re-emerged a century-and-a-half later after the 'worse than Siberian darkness' (Hartmann's phrase) following the battle, a battle which was over after a couple of hours, with fairly small losses, and had evidently not deeply engaged the nation at the time. As Pekař points out, the mercenaries who served on the losing side on the White Mountain cannot be compared to the popular, spontaneous mass rising in support of the Hussites some two centuries earlier. Pekař also believed that though the White Mountain was indeed a national disaster, a Protestant victory, far from preserving Czech culture, would have led to even more effective Germanization than that which occurred under Habsburg and Counter-Reformation auspices. Two rival religions met on the White Mountain – but they were at one in their tendency to Germanize Bohemia. So Pekař believes that the Counter-Reformation actually helped preserve the Czech nation, whereas Patočka focuses on the fact that the Czech nation as we now know it was actually engendered by the Baroque period which followed the battle. Neither the Catholics nor the Protestants celebrate the battle, the issues are too muddled. How could you blend into one commemoration both religious victory and ethnic defeat, or, in the other camp, religious defeat and the creation of the conditions of a rather curious, up-from-below national revival? Could one celebrate submersion so that the situation arises in which one can be reborn so as to be that which one is? One can celebrate a victory or commemorate a defeat, but can one celebrate a nuance of defeat? Rituals are meant to have layers of meaning, but this really would be too much. Prague boasts two panoramas of famous battles, the one terminating the Hussite wars by a fratricidal conflict in which the extremists were defeated and the military aspect of the Hussite adventure was brought to an end, and one commemorating the defence at the very end of the Thirty Years War of the Old Town on Charles Bridge by Catholic students against the Swedes – Protestant allies of Bohemian liberty, but also a band of thieves, who carried away all the art treasures from the castle, which they did manage to capture, even if the students stopped them crossing the stone bridge to the town, and who kept what they looted in Sweden. They betrayed their Bohemian Protestant allies at the peace of Westphalia, not without pocketing some bribes for so doing, a kind of seventeenth-century preview of Munich.

Patočka goes on to characterize modern nationalism as a survival, and comments on how these survivals were very much concentrated in the Habsburg empire. This in a way is strange, for he cannot possibly mean that modern nations are in general continuous with ancient ones (as far as his own nation goes, he holds the opposite view): and in the case of nations 'reborn from below' (like the Czechs), he is only too acutely, and indeed bitterly, aware of the discontinuity, and utterly lucid about the social mechanics of the rebirth, its connection with the urban migration of peasants, and the significance of education for social mobility at a time of political centralization and industrialization. It is curious that Patočka combines the two presumably incompatible views of nationalism, which above all divide theoreticians of nationalism – is it a survival from the past, or is it the fruit of modern conditions? Both, he says. It was by educating peasants, both in the villages and in the towns, that a nation was forged. They were eager to learn, the schoolmaster was the nation-builder, and the professor was to become the national leader. They were obliged to learn, by the conditions prevailing in the world they were entering. This process of education required a history which they could be taught, and this was in due course discovered or invented, in varying proportions. Patočka is probably right in believing that even when this history acquired nominal content or mythology, its real spirit remained that of a Baroque reaction to a menacing, centralizing Enlightenment.

Patočka stresses that, once the overarching unity of medieval Christianity has gone, only idiosyncrasies remain as markers of identity; we are, he says, at home in the accidental and cannot live without it. (Santayana had said much the same: our nationality, like our relations with women, is too deep to be changed honourably and too accidental to be worth changing. As far as Patočka is concerned, they are simply too accidental, not for change, but for elevation to the status of political foundation stones.) Patočka perceives the triangular struggle between this particularism, the Baroque universalism of Maria Theresa, and the new Enlightenment universalism of Joseph II. The new Czech culture, born in the Baroque age, took over the content of Maria Theresa's regime without its intended religious universalism, and benefited politically from the new Enlightenment universalism of her successor, without internalizing its ideas either. So Patočka combines a view of nationalism as a survival from the past, with a more correct perception of the mechanics of its actual emergence under conditions of modernization: the Czech case, though perhaps extreme, is perhaps less atypical than he thinks. Rebirth-from-below may define and accentuate some of its marked features, but its general characteristics pervade the industrial world in any case.

In 1848, the historian Palacký gave the national movement its political direction (which it retained until Masaryk changed tack in 1914); the dynasty had to be persuaded to base itself on the

Slav part of its population. This entails a conservative attitude, which Palacký maintained indeed for the rest of his life, and which earned him the derision of Marx. The Czechs, however, unlike the Magyars, failed in their major efforts to improve their position within the monarchy (indeed they were bound to fail as long as the Hungarians succeeded, for giving in to the Slavs would have meant thwarting the Magyars), and what they learned from their failures was to develop a taste for a tenacious, persistent struggle to win small advantages. In the end, the linguistic programme of the romantics became a reality, Patočka notes, during the epoch of positivism (the 1880s). Linguistically, Charles University underwent binary fission in 1882, and this acquisition of its own educational apex meant the completion of the Czech cultural rebirth, albeit one begun 'from below'. The true succession to the Caroline University continued to be a matter of contention between the Czech and the German heirs: the Germans seized the symbolic insignia after the 1939 occupation of Prague, and, of course, the Czechs abolished the German University altogether in 1945.

Culturally speaking, what sustained this society? 'It is a culture for liberated servants, who are only learning to strive for a greater freedom and their own development. So it is a culture of popular education, it turns to its own society, and not at all to "Man" or "Humanity".' Patočka rejects Masaryk's interpretation of modern Czech history as the continuation of the early Czech Reformation, or the ideals of the Czech Brethren. It should be noted that while he disagrees with Masaryk on history – holding his liberation from historicism to be incomplete, which indeed it was – and observes that Masaryk failed to bring forth even a single new theoretical idea, at the same time he has enormous admiration for his character. Masaryk was a man capable of action and decision, not a mere 'liberated servant'; in other words, he was a counter-example to the pervasive culture, and not merely one more secretary academic. For a Central European professor, Patočka has a refreshing contempt for that combination of petty-bourgeois caution, and Hamletism, in politics or personal life, which would seem to mark us. His admiration for Masaryk is based not on his professorial qualities ('no depth of thought') but on his unprofessorial ones, his awareness of his moral mission and his sense of real problems and his capacity to face them with firmness. It is amusing to think that had the liberation from communism come sooner, or had he lived longer, Patočka himself rather than Havel would have become the professor–president of the freed state, and would have had to face its problems. Suitable professors having run out, however, one had to fall back on a playwright. Would Patočka have dealt more effectively with the Louis-Philippe-style government and the spirit of *enrichissez-vous*?

Masaryk had seen the First World War as the victory of modern democratic states over 'theocratic' regimes based on medieval metaphysics. This never quite fitted the facts, West or East. In the West, Patočka observes, the war was soon seen as a catastrophe and not as a new beginning, as it was among the Czechs. The linguistic nationalism on which it was based proved fatal for their new state, for it alienated the proportionately huge minorities, and within ten years from the end of the war, the world, what with the rise of Stalin and fascisms, came to look quite different from Masaryk's picture. (During the communist period, an essay of Patočka's circulated in *samizdat* in which he pointed out that Nietzsche would have been a better guide and preparation for the age of Hitler and Stalin than the triumphalist rationalism which constituted Masaryk's philosophy.) Then, says Patočka, came the double failure: the Czechs' inability to free themselves from linguistic nationalism, and the inability to defend the democratic state in Central Europe. Beneš, whom Patočka despises, collapsed pathetically when the hour of decision came with Munich, and thereby broke the moral backbone of society. The General Staff told Beneš that the isolated Czech state would be defeated, but that it none the less should be defended, but Beneš surrendered. (This summary of the attitude of the Czech General Staff at the time is not consistent with what can be found in other historical accounts.)

It seems to me that Patočka here ignores at least one part of the logic of Masaryk's heritage: Masaryk taught that it was legitimate to create the state only when given endorsement by world history and the West – he did not distinguish very clearly between the two – and so, would it be right to resist when the West at Munich had pronounced against it? If the West is indeed the mouthpiece and vanguard of world history, and in that capacity is alone entitled to issue warrants for state-formation, then was it not equally entitled, at Munich, to dispense or withdraw permission for defence of the states it had previously authorized? Logically, this would seem to be the case. In his logic if not in his personality, Masaryk had prepared the surrender at Munich. Hence Beneš was merely carrying on the principles of one important aspect of Masaryk's teaching, though Patočka may well be right in suggesting that Masaryk would have acted differently from Beneš in 1938, and might have decided to resist.

Patočka here bitterly repudiates the 1938 surrender, both for its fruits, and its roots, in that small-mindedness which the book is determined to explain historically. The failure springs, he says, from the same sources, from the social structure of Czech society, which seldom and only by accident produces leading personalities, capable of taking radical risk and carrying the burden of enormous responsibility. At the very moment when Patočka preaches the ethic of such total and uncompromising commitment, he slips back into the kind of petty calculation which exemplifies the small-mindedness he denounces: he remarks that, after all, the war might well have been a short one (even though lost), so that, after all, the losses would not have been so disproportionately great. There is something comic in the incommensurability of the two considerations: on the one hand, the commitment to principle at whatever cost (the Hussites had sung *na množství nehleďe*, loosely translated, 'don't count the cost, disregard the numbers') and, on the other, the sly surreptitious calculation that if only we are defeated quickly enough, it won't really cost quite so much. The post-Baroque pettiness seems to blend here with a yearning for pre-White Mountain nobility.

At the very end of the book, Patočka offers a single-paragraph summary of Czech history, in which, curiously, it is once again the (medieval) Bohemian aristocracy which receives a major share of the blame: its limited horizons, its lack of sense of the state, its caprice, carelessness and the irresponsibility, which in the end forced the Habsburgs to reorganize this recalcitrant society (that is, though Patočka does not say so, by bringing in its own men, who leave the indigenous language to the local lower orders, so that when later a linguistically defined nation re-emerges, its restricted recruitment endows it with all the traits Patočka deplores). But for all that, come back Bohemian nobility, all is forgiven, only save us from linguistic nationalism, egalitarianism and petty-mindedness. In fact, the names of the Schwarzenbergs, Lobkowiczs and Kinskys are reappearing in public life. Whether this will have the effect desired by Patočka remains to be seen.

On the surface, Patočka is offering a deep historical explanation of the Munich catastrophe and surrender. But at the time he was writing these lines, another catastrophe, with greater immediate implication for his own situation, was far closer and must be seen as the real basis of his state of mind: the collapse of the Prague Spring of 1968. This remains carefully unmentioned in the text (another example of that spirit of caution he deplores?), but must surely be its real content and the source of its passion. At the time he was writing, Munich was history, but August 1968 was not. It has now also become history, and the consequences of that catastrophe have been corrected, once again gratuitously, from above, by the ruler – not Joseph II this time, but Mikhail Sergeievich Gorbachev – and the nation stands, not on this occasion before a disaster (on the contrary, prospects are good), but a parting of the ways, between the claustro-philia and focus on petty aims which seem to characterize the first government of the new Czech republic, and a more generous and global spirit, exemplified by Havel. Patočka's book is formally about 1938 (explaining it, among other factors, by the moral defects of late medieval barons), but in reality about 1968. It was after all written at the very height of post-Spring 'normalization'. But it has a curiously powerful resonance in 1993, during the emergence of the first Czech, as opposed to Czechoslovak, government.

11

The Nazi Jew-lover

The twentieth century is marked amongst other things by the prominence of a distinctive kind of expiation literature – the disavowal of totalitarian tyranny and ideology by men whose sin was to have supported it.* Each of the two great ideocratic dictatorships dominated extensive territory for a time, and also had its impact beyond the boundaries of its rule, and secured the adherence of numerous intellectuals, both by conviction and by coercion, or some combination of the two. Each of them collapsed ignominiously, found wanting by a court of its own choice: the Nazis believed in war and were defeated in war, the Bolsheviks believed that the secret of human history lay in the growth of productive forces, and they were eliminated by self-confessed defeat in an economic race. After the collapse, and often before it, those who lost their erstwhile faith or were freed by circumstance from the obligation to subscribe to it, were put in a situation in which they had to face the question – why did I support a system guilty of such appalling crimes?

Hjalmar Schacht, the banker who helped devise the partially Keynesian system which sustained the Nazi economy, proudly

* Hugo Ott (1993), *Martin Heidegger: An Intellectual and Political Portrait.* Basic Books, New York.
Hans Sluga, *Heidegger's Crisis: Philosophy and Politics in Nazi Germany.*

settled his score with Hitler by publishing a book with that very title – *Abrechnung mit Hitler* – when the Führer was safely dead. Schacht can also be seen on surviving news-reels of 1940, ecstatically and interminably shaking Hitler's hand by way of congratulating him on the great victory in the Battle of France. It must have hurt Adolf's hand, who I imagine wished the sycophantic banker were not quite so effusive. Had Hitler won, Schacht would have kept his *Abrechnung* to himself. When I attend conferences of thinkers on the continent of Europe (which is quite often), usually dedicated to topics such as liberalism or democracy, one game I tend to play inwardly when bored is to survey the participants, and ask myself – how many, and which ones, would also be here, in the same place, discussing the Regeneration of Europe under the Nazis, had the war gone the other way? Of course I wouldn't be there to see them, but it is an amusing game and it has kept me awake through some boring speeches or papers.

The involvements of intellectuals in the two great dictatorships, however, are not altogether symmetrical. The literature of expiatory de-Bolshevization is much richer than that of de-Nazification. The Bolsheviks had a much longer run than the Nazis: there is quite a difference between 70 and 12 years. Nazism contained an important anti-intellectual element: what counts is warm blood not cold reason. So, even if intellectual support or conformity was required, it was also implicitly or openly despised. By contrast, the Marxists believed in the Unity of Theory and Practice, which meant in practice that political leaders had to pretend to be abstract theorists and their works had to be treated with respect. Doctrine was codified with a thoroughness and completeness probably seldom rivalled since the days of high scholasticism. Equally important, or perhaps more so, the basic moral values underlying Marxism – universal brotherhood of man and human fulfilment without exploitation or oppression – can continue to be upheld without shame: the erstwhile believer can claim that it was the implementation and not the moral intuition which was wrong, even if the implementation was the inevitable consequence of certain aspects of the doctrine ('we failed to see that'). Thinkers such as Arnošt Kolman or Adam Schaf could write along such lines long after the horrors of communism had ceased to be contentious.

By contrast, the Nazi salvation was selective, it was reserved for the strong and victorious, and when they lost, there was no logical bolthole. Either way, they were wrong, whether one appeals to the laws of humanity or the law of the jungle. Consequence: ex-commies write mea culpa books, ex-Nazis in the main retire into amnesia. With the final collapse of 'real socialism', a new brand of ex-commie emerges, who had stayed with the system not from deep conviction but from an acceptance of its strength and local inevitability, and when history surprisingly but conclusively refuted the Inescapability thesis, once again there is no escape, and the survivor may resemble the ex-Nazis: converted in theory to economic ultra-liberalism and in practice to mafioso capitalism, he won't write any books either. Alternatively, the book will be about *realpolitik* rather than about Marxism. If I may name-drop: on the one occasion when I had dinner with the Pope, I asked him what he thought of Jaruzelski, then still in power. The answer was interesting: Jaruzelski was, His Holiness observed, a military man: it was no use discussing Marxist philosophy with him, *he does not know much about it!* The Pope, who, whatever one may think of his social policies, does genuinely like philosophy, and he could probably run rings around the General when it comes to discussing the dialectic of history. When the General's memoirs become properly available, we may hope for some illumination concerning recent history, but we need expect no contribution to the labour theory of value.

This silence, especially on the part of ex-Nazis, may be a pity, in as far as we need to understand the Gods that Failed, and amongst these failed gods, one is very much better endowed with literary post-mortems than the other. Yet both these totalitarianisms had deep roots in European thought and experience, notably in the reaction to the Enlightenment and attempts at its implementation in Europe. (North America was more fortunate: in a society already endowed with many of the features required by the Enlightenment, even before it was codified, an enlightened

Constitution could be drafted and made to work without too much political turbulence: not so on the continent of Europe.) The great paradox of Marxism is that it was born of the insight that society cannot just be re-ordered in accordance with an enlightened blueprint, one has to allow for the realities and constraints of inherited social organization and its productive base. In the course of implementing this idea, by fusing all economic, political and ideological hierarchies in a single monopolistic system, the eventual collapse of the system is forcing its heirs to cope, precisely, with something closer to a social *tabula rasa* than other reformers have ever had to face. The experiment had engendered the very thing it has deemed impossible. By contrast, Nazism was curiously pluralist, tolerating and using many inherited institutions and ideas. To my knowledge, there is no clear formulation of the ideas which inspired it.

But the ideas were there, and one can try and get them clear. Nazism was not something which had crawled out from under the floorboards, as Hannah Arendt had claimed (from a possibly unconscious attempt to exonerate her ex-lover Martin Heidegger). It too was in part an attempt to complete the Enlightenment, and in part a reaction to it. It took seriously the view that man was part of nature, which in practice meant that in assessing his real satisfactions and values, one had to pay more attention to his drives (e.g. aggression, domination) than abstract, cerebral, resentment-engendered ideals of universalism and equality. (This, in simple terms, is part of the Nietzschean use of Darwin.) These misguided Judaeo-Christian values, perpetuated by the Enlightenment in a secular idiom, had to be sloughed off. This rejection of universalism was blended with another one, the communalistic stress on *Gemeinschaft*, which stresses that which is specific in individual cultures rather than that which is all-human, as well as accepting the closed and hierarchical nature of the community in which men found their true fulfilment. The community was to be seen as biological as well as cultural (or rather, the two aspects were to be linked to each other), and conflict and ruthlessness were the conditions of excellence and perpetuation of the community so conceived.

This vision, however much one rejects it, is important and its historical incarnation, the nature of its appeal and its actual consequences, is something which needs to be understood. From this viewpoint, the significance of Martin Heidegger is that he is widely acclaimed as the most important German philosopher of his time, that he was involved in Nazism (though the extent and nature of the involvement are contentious), and that he had ample time, before, during and after the Nazi period, to reflect and write on the matter.

Heidegger's location in the history of philosophy lies at the intersection of phenomenology and existentialism. He was a pupil and disciple of the Jewish thinker Edmund Husserl, who invented phenomenology, and he added a strong existentialist twist to the tradition. Phenomenology consists of focusing on objects of our thought *as we actually think them*, i.e. eschewing the 'natural viewpoint' (in fact: the natural viewpoint of a scientific age), which consists of assuming that everything is really explained in terms of something else, something more elementary and general. This twist provided philosophy with a new sphere of investigation, and incidentally legitimated and christened the *Lebenswelt*, the world-as-lived. Once upon a time, there had been no other world, and the lived-world needed neither a name nor a defence, but nowadays, since the impact of science, all this has kind of changed.

Existentialism adds to this a preoccupation with the human condition, the predicament of man 'thrown into the world'. Add to this a preoccupation with ancient Greek thought, from a vantage point much influenced by Nietzsche. (In a text published in French in 1966 and in German in 1969, 'The End of Philosophy and the Task of Thinking', Heidegger links Nietzsche – and Marx – to the attainment of 'the most extreme possibility of philosophy' – but it seems that something remains still to be done. His prose explaining what that residue is, is impenetrable.) Socratic rationalism can be seen as a danger to vitality analogous to that presented by modern rationalism, and on the other hand, Greek preoccupation with being as such can be invoked as a corrective to the merely specialized or technological, instrumental aspects of modern thought, or of the kind of epistemology-centred modern thought which focuses on man-the-alien-investigator, ignoring the fact that man is already *in* the world, a troubled citizen or even an anguished prisoner, and not a foreign, detached and intellectual spy, which is what Descartes had tried to make him. Something along these lines is the cocktail provided by Heidegger. As no one would accuse him of being the world's most lucid writer, it is hard to be sure that one has got it absolutely right.

A priori, does this kind of philosophizing lend itself to use as a charter of Nazism? The answer is not obvious. There would seem to be an overlap in what is being rejected, but not in what is positively asserted (not to mention the embarrassment of its Jewish origin). The Nazis, or some of them, had their doubts about him, from their own viewpoint: 'Heidegger's thought is characterised by the same obsession with hairsplitting distinctions as Talmudic thought. This is why it holds such extraordinary fascination for Jews, persons of Jewish ancestry and others with a similar mental make-up.' (So wrote one Erich Jaensch in 1934, as quoted in Ott's book, p. 257.)

Hugo Ott's book, whose original publication in German caused a stir, provides a great deal of detailed and convincing material concerning Heidegger's institutional involvement with Nazism, and de-Nazification. Anyone interested in the facts will find a mass of them assembled and documented here. That there had been such involvement is scarcely in doubt, and has not been in doubt for a considerable time. Yet the picture remains murky. The author disclaims philosophical schooling and says he does not really deal with Heidegger's position in the history of philosophy. But is that not of the essence? I for one sympathize with Heidegger's own remark, cited by Ott, that his life is uninteresting, and that only the work matters – or rather, I would add, the implications and impact of that work. Ott also explicitly refrains from dealing with the episode in Heidegger's life which perhaps is best known in America, namely his involvement with Hannah Arendt. (On her account, she was *the* love of his life. One thing at any rate is certain: there were no Nuremberg Laws restricting access to Martin Heidegger's bed.) The material, though very interesting, is presented in an untidy and jerky way – perhaps because it was originally assembled for separate articles. There is no summary of the institutional or ideological context within which the various episodes occur, which would help an outsider to make sense of it all.

If there is a general conclusion, it would seem to be that Heidegger was unquestionably guilty of involvement in Nazism (something which has hardly been in doubt, but perhaps had not been so well documented), but that the sinner had perhaps inwardly returned to the bosom of the Catholic Church, or in any case would have been warmly welcome. This theme haunts the book, as a kind of counterpoint to the demonstrated involvement in Nazism – but the evidence for it is, by comparison, shadowy. For instance, in 1945, at a time when the French military authorities ruled in the area, Heidegger contemplated organizing a seminar on the thought of Blaise Pascal. (It never came off.) Ott notes correctly that this was 'a clever tactical move', but goes on to ask whether it was not also (given Heidegger's awareness of Pascal's devotion to the God of Abraham) a sign of a religious (re)conversion? This is thin evidence indeed. Many of us conduct seminars on thinkers whose religious commitment does not tempt us. Incidentally, the French, though suspicious of Heidegger, were planning to arrange a meeting between him and Sartre as early as November 1945, with a view to possible lectures on existentialism in France itself. Ott doesn't tell us whether any such meeting took place, and omits to say that Heidegger evidently did not reciprocate Sartre's respect, and once referred to Sartre's most ambitious philosophical work as 'dreck' (a term somewhat half-way between dirt and shit), as reported in Bryan Magee's *The Great Philosophers* (1987, p. 275).

A somewhat sentimental epilogue more insistently insinuates a hypothetical terminal reconciliation with the Church, whilst candidly admitting that the question of whether such a return occurred is 'by no means easy'. The evidence for a positive conclusion is restricted to what *others*, not Heidegger himself, have said, more by way of hope or piety than of observation, and the fact that, though the cross is absent from the headstone, the cross carved on the near-by graves of kin, 'appears to be touching the philosopher's grave as well' (*sic*). Evidence of such kind is a good deal less than convincing, though the author seems keen to establish not merely that Heidegger was a sinner, but also that he may be a redeemed one. In an earlier passage, however, whilst describing how Heidegger sought the aid of the Church in his struggle for rehabilitation, after failing to secure adequate help from Karl Jaspers, he notes that there could be no reconciliation between Heidegger's secular philosophizing and religious dogma. Heidegger himself blamed the Church for blocking full rehabilitation at one stage.

Ott asks in so many words whether Heidegger was the Prodigal Son, but then answers in a manner which can only be described as ambiguous, yet intended to encourage hope in those who wish for an affirmative answer. The question does not seem to me to be the most important one. The general conclusion of Ott's book is that Heidegger was indubitably guilty, but that we may hope in the end he was redeemed by his ancestral faith. One who loved his own roots so much, and was so devoted to the pursuit of truth, would surely return to the fold . . . That seems to be the message, though admittedly it is conveyed without dogmatism, tentatively. He certainly loved his roots; I am not so sure about the other premise of this questionable argument.

To read Ott's book is to eavesdrop on a German intra-family debate. A black sheep of the family is being discussed, his sins taken a little more seriously than they deserve, because his international fame causes his record to reflect more on the family's good name than would otherwise be the case; but the content of his work is barely considered and a vast amount of background is simply taken for granted. Hans Sluga's book is quite different, and it makes up for many of Ott's deficiencies. Though judging from the name and occasional stylistic idiosyncracies, this Berkeley professor is German (the surname suggests an ultimate Polish origin), he is much less concerned with proving to himself or others that Heidegger's soul was saved in the end, and instead sets himself the laudable task of clarifying the political, institutional and philosophical context in which it all happened. In this he is very successful, though I am not sure whether someone without previous knowledge of the field will be all that much wiser after reading the summaries of philosophical positions. But perhaps, given the limitations of an elegantly slim volume, that would be asking too much.

Sluga's book provides a lot of very interesting information. For instance, there were roughly 180 philosophers holding appointments in 1933, and of these, only a dozen were members of the Nazi party. Thirty joined that year, and 40 joined later, so that almost half were members by 1940. Given the fact that the German university system, especially at that time, cannot easily be translated into say the American one, it would have been useful if 'appointment' were carefully defined: does it include junior ranks not yet properly paid?

The general picture offered by Sluga is convincing. The philosophical situation during the Weimar period was untidy and it remained such thereafter: there was no effective *Gleichschaltung* in this sphere. There was no philosophical codification of Nazism, and Heidegger certainly didn't attempt anything of the kind, let alone provide it. Likewise, he offered no retrospective account after the debacle. On both counts, his position was not idiosyncratic, but on the contrary, typical of the wider intellectual climate, passing from compliance to amnesia.

Sluga does not think that the Nazis had any philosophy. As far as superficial evidence is concerned, no doubt this is correct: there is no codified credo. It is extremely interesting to learn that Hitler, very late in his life, still observed that freedom of inquiry obtained in the natural sciences, and that philosophy was an extension of those sciences. A charismatic leader makes do without charismatic doctrine, at least in formal philosophy. In a deeper sense, there was a coherent cluster of values and ideas – nationalism, biologism, communalism, hierarchy, corporatism, acceptance of authority, territoriality, aggression, rejection of compassion – which governed the policies of the regime. This cluster did not simply spring out of the head of Hitler, it has its roots in European history and ideas, and deserves investigation, even if the

Nazis did not make it easier for us by leaving behind a corpus of authoritative texts.

Sluga's own philosophical position inspires his *Fragestellung* but does not obscure the story. Although in fact he condemns the German philosophical generation(s) in question, his own grapplings with the relationship of philosophy and politics lead him towards a relativism which would make it hard ever to judge one period by the standards of another. He comes close to saying, not so much that the past is another country, but that it is beyond judgement. Ethics look to the future: this view, once elaborated so as to make value judgements compatible with determinism (moral judgements make sense in a determined world just because they have an effect on the future), seems here to be used to abolish retrospective morality. So whereas for Ott, Heidegger may be saved by a secret return to his ancestral faith, for Sluga he may benefit from a universal philosophical amnesty, granted to the past as such. Perhaps Sluga, who has previously worked on Frege – revered as crucial founder of modern logic, but a rabid racist and early Nazi – will eventually expound these rather strange views, indebted both directly and by reaction to Nietzsche and Foucault, somewhere else: here they helped him organize the narrative, but happily do not cloud it.

My own regret is not that Heidegger was involved in Nazism at all, but that his involvement is so wobbly – whether *for* or *against* it. By this I do not mean that I wish Heidegger had gone about, at the time the stormtroopers were breaking windows of Jewish shops, breaking the windows of the offices of Jewish professors (instead of helping to exclude some, whilst aiding others, for instance to obtain posts abroad). Nor do I wish he had been more eager to join the *Volksturm* during that final agony of the Third Reich, instead of being anxious to evade such service and protesting against it – though I am a bit surprised that one who attributed such importance to the facing of death and nothingness in the forging of human identity, should not have welcomed the opportunity for intimate confrontation with it. Perhaps, if the void is ever with us, one need not seek it out with excessive zeal.

It is interesting that other extreme romantics of roughly similar mould, such as Ernst Juenger – who had done so well in the first war and had evidently found it a most rewarding experience, but preferred cultural liaison work in the second – or Ernst von Solomon, who once combined *Freikorps* service and the perpetration of political murder for the Fatherland with eager study of the works of Walter Rathenau whom he helped murder – can romanticism go further? you *read* rather than eat your victim – and who left us an incomparably more vivid account of what it was like to be a German nationalist under the Nazis, and to have a Jewish mistress into the bargain, than anything found in Heidegger – both behaved similarly.

What I do mean is that a more vigorous involvement, one way or the other, even if he changed his mind, would have taught us more about the options of European thought and feeling at the time, than can be gleaned from these ambiguities and vacillations. He was enthusiastic about the German resurgence, continued to refer to it even after the end of his active involvement in the Party, but changed references to it in post-war publications of the earlier work, somewhat comically, turning 'the inward truth and greatness of National Socialism' into 'the inward truth and greatness of the movement' (namely with the encounter between technology on a planetary scale and modern man). The text is re-edited so as to replace Nazism by some kind of benign ecological concern. Yet he also claimed to have been the critic of those who implemented that resurgence. In fact he was a Nazi for a time and claimed to have been their critic later, but the trouble is that his pro-Nazi statements, about national revival, are banal, whilst his anti-Nazi ones seem non-existent. Either way, one learns nothing about the dilemmas of the time. Those who hold him to be a great thinker may be pained by his involvement. To me it is a matter of indifference: it is less than obvious that he had the stature which would endow the question with great importance.

It is by contrast a matter of deep significance that Andrei Sakharov, for instance, a truly great, brilliant and humane man, was once able to support the Stalinist system, whilst knowing full well how it treated slave labour. *That* is an important and troubling question. That it should have been possible is disturbing. On the other hand, I don't really care what Heidegger got up to. After all this time, I find Heidegger's involvement in Nazism, real though it is, rather boring and unilluminating. Unlike the author of the first book under review, to whom it clearly matters a good deal, and whom it evidently drove both into thorough probing of archives and into anxious speculation, I don't greatly care whether Heidegger was or was not a Nazi, or indeed whether or not in the deepest recesses of his soul in the end he made some kind of equivocal peace with the Church. His involvement was sordid rather than demonic or tragic, and above all, it lacks incisiveness and character, intellectually as well as morally. Why even compare a hero with a petty sinner, you may ask. The point is, not that Sakharov is simply in a totally different class morally or as a scientist, but that even in the field which is central for Heidegger, philosophy, and merely a side-line for Sakharov, I still find Sakharov superior. And in the present context, what is relevant is the light they throw on the confrontation between intellectuals and totalitarian, ideologically monopolistic power.

Given the difficulty of the situation and the strength of the contending forces in Heidegger's breast, and his milieu, I find his hesitations more forgivable than the low quality or paucity of the comments they inspire. I am not put off by the Hamlet-like vacillations, but rather, by the fact that in the course of them, he tells me little or nothing of interest concerning that which attracts or frightens him. By contrast, Sakharov's moral crises are real, his thought is about the real world, and even or especially his personal love is much more convincing. It profoundly influenced his politics (much to the irritation of some of his compatriots, who quite specially resented the impact of an ethnically un-kosher attachment – how dare a Jewish–Armenian woman take over a Russian sage? – so here there is a certain parallel), whilst Heidegger's love life, for all his romanticism, seems more in the nature of a hobby than anything else. The conflict between his sex life and the legal impositions of the Movement which he had declared to be a national regeneration, does not seem to have inspired any profound thoughts. Curious. So, when it comes to

Heidegger's involvements, at any of these levels, I feel more in the presence of an interplay of romantic play-acting and opportunism than of thought. They tell us little about Nazism or philosophy or European history.

Or, if the comparison with Sakharov (whom, quite apart from his distinction as a dissident-liberator and as a physicist, I find more interesting simply as a philosopher than I do Heidegger) is held to be too exacting, how about comparing him with Jan Patočka, the Czech philosopher and eventually dissident, whose reflections on the historic roots of the crisis of his own nation, its failure to resist either Nazism or communism, came out this year (*Was sind die Tschechen?*, Prague, 1993.) Morally, here too there is no comparison: Patočka ended as an unambiguous resister of totalitarianism. But intellectually, the juxtaposition is entirely appropriate: Patočka's intellectual background is virtually identical with Heidegger's. Both were phenomenologists and longstanding, careful students and pupils of Edmund Husserl (though I do not know whether Patočka, like Heidegger, failed to attend Husserl's funeral); and both were preoccupied with ancient Greek thought and with Nietzsche (Patočka went as far as to suggest, in an essay which had to appear in samizdat at the time, that Nietzsche would have been a better guide for the Czechs in modern times than Masaryk). But though I find Patočka's purely philosophical writings almost as difficult as Heidegger's, his historical reflections, in the work cited, are incisive and to the point and meaty, whether or not one agrees with them. Is there anything to compare with this in the work of Heidegger? Instead, one finds bizarre but confident prophecies: for instance, in a text first published in 1966, he claims that cybernetics is about to take over the human sciences. 'No prophecy is required to recognize that the sciences now establishing themselves will soon be determined and steered by the new fundamental science which is called cybernetics. This science corresponds to the determination of man as an acting social being.' The critic of the instrumental–technological vision seems prone to accept exaggerated and premature claims made on its behalf at face value.

When an overall assessment of the involvement of intellectuals

with totalitarianisms comes to be made, the Heidegger dossier
will be there amongst the relevant evidence, and the contents of
these books will form part of it. But Heidegger will not be present
as a significant contributor to the debate. That would seem to
me to be the case against being too interested in him.

12

The Mightier Pen:
The Double Standards of
Inside-out Colonialism

European imperialism of the eighteenth and nineteenth centuries, formally dismantled in the twentieth but surviving in many forms, is in certain important ways unique. It wasn't simply a matter of one set of people dominating others, it involved a move from one kind of society to a profoundly different one. It is this deep metamorphosis and the difficulty of finding a viewpoint from which to judge it, which is the real problem of imperialism. It cannot be seen in terms of imperialist-baddies and resister-goodies. No amount of restraint or tolerance on the part of the rulers, no amount of pride, conservatism and stubbornness on the part of the ruled, could avoid at least some measure of a transvaluation of values. By what standards can we judge this? Like the emperor who found Rome brick and left it marble, these conquerors found the world agrarian and left it industrial, or poised to become such. This raises tremendous problems. Their solution is in no way advanced by inventing a bogy called Orientalism – and still less by the insinuation that if the bogy is overcome, all will be made plain.

Note that not one, but at least two overlapping and distinctive cultural contrasts are involved in the process of modern imperialism and of the subsequent decolonization. There is the generic difference between agrarian and industrial society; and there is the difference between 'Western' society and the residue of human societies. The two contrasts are independent of each other: we do not know which of the many characteristics of Western societies bestowed on them their temporary predominance. Westerners themselves credited their election, at various times, to Christianity, rationalism, individualism, capitalism, virtue, genes, Marxism, Protestantism, valour, constitutionalism, democracy; and no doubt there have been other candidates. In the course of their domination, social traits of the dominators which may have been totally irrelevant to the situation benefited from a free ride: for instance, European soldiers wore fairly narrow rather than baggy trousers, and modernizing-Westernizing Muslim rulers imitated this sartorial feature, much to the irritation of their own soldiers, who were less smitten by an uncritical general yearning for the West. So they rolled up their trousers in defiance of the West and of their own officers. However, this does not mean that tight trousers are an absolutely essential constituent of human progress; nor does it mean that baggy trousers advance cultural fulfilment.

Moreover, over and above the fact that the industrial/agrarian and Western/Other distinctions cut across each other, and obscure each other's outline, we have by now an additional one which cuts across both: there is a difference between the social and cultural traits which favour advanced industrialism, and those which had made its emergence possible in the first place, before its potential was properly understood. The brilliant economic success of some Far Eastern societies suggests that whereas Calvinist individualism may have favoured the initial appearance of the new order, once it has come into being, and its advantages are clear to all, it can better be run in a Confucian–collectivist spirit. This isn't yet fully established, but it constitutes a distinct possibility.

It is against this background that one has to face the problem of the cultural interaction set off by imperial expansion. What can justify or vindicate the stance which one adopts? If there is, anywhere in Edward Said's *Culture and Imperialism*, a discussion of this problem, it has entirely escaped me. Said's own values, as expressed in the culminating passages of the book, are unexceptionable:

No one today is purely *one* thing. Labels like Indian, or woman, or American, are no more than starting points. . . . Imperialism consolidated the mixture of cultures and identities on a global scale. But its worst and most paradoxical gift was to allow people to believe that they were only, mainly, exclusively, white, or black, or western, or Oriental. Yet . . . [n]o one can deny the persisting continuities of long traditions . . . but there seems no reason except fear and prejudice to keep insisting on their separation and distinctiveness, as if that was all human life was about . . . this also means not trying to rule others, not trying to classify them or put them into hierarchies.

Amen. It would be hard to dissent from the underlying moral current of this: we are all human and should treat each other decently and with respect. Don't take more specific classifications seriously. Is categorization between consenting adults to be allowed to all?

But still, there are some things wrong even with this anodyne expression of our shared pieties. Was it really imperialism which first imposed rigid classifications on people? Deeply internalized, socially enforced distinctions between categories of people constituted a general characteristic of complex societies. They were only loosened and partly eroded by that modern turbulence which brought in its train, but is not exhausted by, 'imperialism'. Mobility, egalitarianism and free choice of identity have better prospects in the modern world than they had in the past. Should there not, on the part of one who seems to value this free, individualist choice of identity, be at least some expression of gratitude towards the process which has made such a free choice so much easier – even if it also for a time engendered an initial disparity of power between early and later beneficiaries of modernity?

Another way of putting it would be to say that Said's entire approach is based on four assumptions: (1) the recent domination of the world by the West can be seen as an event in its own right, rather than as primarily an aspect of the transformation of the world by a new technology, economy and science – which happens, owing to the uneven nature of its diffusion, to engender a temporary and unstable imbalance of power; (2) the cruelties

and injustices which take place between early and late beneficiaries of the new power are somehow worse or more reprehensible
than those which customarily take place *within* either traditional
or modernized societies; (3) these inequalities are reflected in the
culture and literatures of the societies affected, which deserves
attentive investigation; and (4) these cultural aspects of the imbalance of power were essential to it, and not mere superficial
accompaniments. Of the four assumptions, (1), (2) and (4) seem
to me at the very least questionable and probably false, whereas
(3) is unquestionably sound. The trouble is, Said doesn't even
seriously raise, let alone answer, questions concerning (1) and
(2); one must gladly concede (3); and as to (4), he emphatically
affirms it, but fails to establish it. I have grave doubts about
it.

The book offers no general discussion of the nature of cultural
transformation, or contact and conflict of values, nor does it offer
a theory of how, given competing viewpoints, we can legitimately
claim objectivity for our own moral or cognitive stance. Nineteenth-
century evolutionism, which Said repudiates, offered an ingenious solution, which on the one hand recognized cultural variety,
yet on the other provided a basis for judgement: cultures were
ranked on an evolutionary ladder, and the upward struggle along
it endowed life and history with meaning. All cultures were legitimate but later ones more so. This imposed a ranking on cultures, which is unacceptable to Said, though ranking, as such,
can be separated from the Eurocentric versions once prevalent,
and a non-Eurocentric form of the theory may yet find favour.

The prevalent mood of expiation for empire is often associated
with a wild subjectivism, which would happily endorse *all* cultures (which leads to a contradiction, by endorsing the ethnocen-
tric absolutism found within so many of them). Said never goes
that far: there is no shrill 'postmodernist' pan-relativism in his
book. He simply makes himself a present of a stance from which
he can pass moral judgement and tell us how things really stand,
without facing the difficulties of validating it. If the colonialists
were victims of their cultural situation, what warrant is there for
Said's own cultural location? Having rejected evolutionist ranking,

yet without espousing the voguish relativism which blesses everything (in practice, selectively), Said is left with an objectivism which hangs in thin air, without support, but allows him to explain and put down the 'Orientalists', and reduce their vision to the allegedly important role it played in world domination.

I fear that this kind of unsustained, facile inverse colonialism has grave dangers for the moral sensibility of anyone practising it: for instance, genuine and outstanding scholars who have made important contributions to the understanding of non-Western societies, without the least touch of condescension (for instance, Bernard Lewis, Patricia Crone, Michael Cook) are unfairly denounced; by contrast, Said accepts someone like Thomas Hodgkin, who practised a kind of inside-out Blimpery, and mechanically endorsed and underwrote a catastrophic and comic Third World dictator, Nkrumah, simply because he spoke radical and was not Western. Hodgkin is repeatedly invoked as if he were a serious witness concerning the correct relationship between East and West, or North and South. Said fails to see that the double standard implied in the tacitly patronizing attitude of such men (tenderly condoning sins in their heroes which would be excoriated at home) is far more genuinely and deeply insulting than a dispassionate analysis of other cultures.

Said incidentally lets off the founding fathers of Marxism far too easily. It is not enough to refer to 'their theories of Oriental and African ignorance and superstition'. Without ever formally systematizing it, Marx and Engels came very close to having two distinct theories of history, one for Europe, the other for the Rest. In the West, all class-endowed societies are in the end said to be unstable and bound to perish through their own contradictions, so guaranteeing eventual salvation; in the East, genuine stagnation is possible and obtains, as does the primacy of coercion over production, which inhibits the liberation of mankind through growth of productive forces and the consequent adjustments in society. So the East can only be liberated by courtesy of the West. This Eurocentrism continued, for instance, to be markedly present in Sartre, who, though supposed to be on the side of the angels, considered the dialectic to be a European speciality, extended to others by courtesy – a kind of *mission dialectisante*, or Left Bank's Burden? – and he was rightly rebuked for this by Lévi-Strauss. Eurocentric blinkers are not restricted to the political right.

So Said does not really face the problems of moral–historical accountancy in the transformation of the world, yet allows himself judgements which presuppose that these questions have been answered. If he evades yet prejudges the general issues, how does he fare on details? I have had a special look at his extensive handling of North Africa, partly because my own ignorance is less complete in this field than elsewhere, and partly because the interface of two confident cultures, Arab and French, each with a tendency to absolutize itself (each believes its own language to reflect the true order of things), does indeed present a marvellous and revealing example of cultural confrontation, and Said rightly gives it much attention.

Looking at the manner in which he handles this theme, I am struck by how much is left out, how much is misleading and how much is mistaken. André Gide naturally makes his appearance. *L'Immoraliste* is a gift to anyone pursuing this theme, and Gide himself a sitting duck: few men have more shamelessly used another country as a name for their own fantasy. No doubt it was easier to find attractive homosexual partners in Biskra than among the *haute bourgeoisie protestante*, but this does not mean that the Algerian oasis was a residue of ancient Mediterranean sensuous harmony, liberty and fulfilment. Said here fails to pursue his quarry as it deserves to be pursued, and misses out on how terribly wrong Gide was, how shamelessly he used Algeria for a projection based on his own need. Said fails to show up Gide fully because, like Gide, he also is more interested in his own theme than in the Algerians. In *L'Immoraliste*, and in *Si le grain ne meurt* for that matter, Gide's underlying argument is: it was northern Protestantism which forced me, Gide, to deny my true nature and my fulfilment, a Protestantism symbolized by those dreadful pines and the declamatory landscape and puritanism of the Swiss Alps. But ah! as I move south, things improve, they get quite nice in southern Italy, and the final release takes place among the palm trees of Biskra, where an Apollonian shrine consecrates a liberated spirit. Gide adapted and eroticized the hymn to Nature found in that compendium of Enlightenment, d'Holbach's *System of Nature*, to convey his vision.

Gide is entitled to his personal parables. But what a travesty of the realities! At the very moment he was celebrating his own sensuous liberation, a movement was starting, not at all far from Biskra (one leader came from that very region, and another from an adjoining area a little to the north), destined to turn Algeria into the Eire of the Muslim world, a nation whose identity was forged around a severely puritan, scripturalist version of an old faith, previously held in a more relaxed, quasi-pagan spirit. But even if one took the unreformed version of Algerian culture, it hardly exemplifies the kind of free, naturalistic fulfilment Gide commended: one much admired traditional folk-hero of the Kabyles, for instance, is a man who kills his own daughter for unchastity; a display of the virtue of a Roman judge, but at the service of purity rather than justice, if indeed such a distinction can be drawn.

Said fails to exploit properly the disparity between Gide's self-indulgent projection and Algerian reality because he himself is more concerned with his general thesis – literature at the service of colonialism, or of resistance to it – than with the concrete society with which he is dealing. Ben Badis, the puritan reformer who really forged the modern Algerian moral climate and identity (and whose base was a little north of Biskra, in Constantine), is not even mentioned. Instead, there is a lot about Frantz Fanon. Here, Said misses the point that Fanon was for export only: influential though he no doubt was in the internationally literary–intellectual scene, he meant nothing to the Algerians themselves. Ben Badis, unknown internationally, meant a very great deal. The Algerian war, lost on the ground, was won in the arena of international opinion, and here Fanon was invaluable; but he made no contribution to the content of Algerian life or thought. Said, commendably, doesn't care for nationalism too much, and hopes that decolonization will lead to something better; and he finds support in Fanon's views:

[Fanon's] notion was that unless national consciousness at its moment of success is somehow changed into social consciousness, the future would hold not liberations but an extension of imperialism. . . . The struggle must be lifted to a new level of contest, a synthesis represented by a war of liberation, for which an entirely new post-nationalism theoretical culture is required.

How this could relate to reality is less than clear. Certainly, nothing of the kind happened. On the ground, the Algerians turned, not to a 'new post-nationalist theoretical culture', but to fundamentalism, which in the Muslim context plays the same social role as nationalism does in Europe: it provides men deprived of their niche in the old stable local structures with an identity in a High Culture, one that confers dignity. Said misdescribes the process: 'In Algeria . . . the French forbade Arabic as a formal language of instruction or administration; after 1962 the FLN made it understandably the only such language. . . . The FLN then proceeded politically to absorb the whole of Algerian civil society.'

None of this is right. The moral climate of Muslim Algeria was transformed during the earlier part of the century by a Reformist puritan movement led by Ben Badis. The movement did use Arabic as its language of instruction, and Arabic was also not absent from the so-called Franco-Muslim *lycées*. Nor was the FLN able, immediately after its victory in 1962, to reverse the situation. Arabic was installed fairly soon in areas which don't matter too much (justice, the humanities), but not in areas which do matter (the sciences, oil, real administration). The completion of the Arabization process was the fruit of a long, costly and heroic *Kulturkampf*, comparable to the Hebraicization of Israel, and similarly motivated, by a national imperative. The Algerians succeeded where the less powerfully motivated Irish failed. The Irish secured puritanism but not the recovery of the national language; the Algerians attained both.

It is also quite untrue that the FLN ever absorbed the whole of Algerian civil society. It monopolized what mattered (state, army, large-scale economy) and left moral legitimacy to the new petty bourgeoisie, which had replaced the *pieds-noirs*, and to reformist religion. This division of labour eventually failed, and a civil society of a characteristically Muslim kind, without political power, but with independent control of the ultimate (religious) sources of legitimacy, in the end dared turn against the technocrats–janissaries. It won the elections, and it may yet win power. Anyone taking his picture of the Algerian cultural and political development from Said would be badly misled. Said also blames Camus for claiming that the Algerian nation had never existed, but omits to say that this remark had also been made by Ferhat Abbas, the nominal (though not effective) leader during the run-up to victory of the Algerian FLN movement.

It is strange how very much Said misses out. There is no mention, for instance, of a moving account of what it felt like to be an Algerian Muslim, namely Malek Bennabi's *Témoin du siècle*. The most intriguing nineteenth-century case of the pursuit of identity, Ismail Urbain, half-French, half-Caribbean and champion of Algerian Muslims under Louis Napoleon, and thus a clear predecessor of Fanon, does not appear. Nor does Ch. R. Ageron's standard and excellent work on the Algerians under French rule. Jacques Berque's memoirs, a splendid account of what it was to be a *pied-noir* slowly converted to anti-colonialism, is likewise absent. That book conveys the intercultural sexuality ('the two communities only met in the *Quartier reservé*') and a sense of provinciality. Unlike Camus, and despite his anti-colonialist metaphysics, Berque was never fully incorporated by the Paris mandarins, even with a professorship at the Collège de France. No sign either of Ali Merad's two remarkable books on the Reformist movement which totally transformed Algerian culture, in effect created Algerian identity, and made the revolution possible; yet Said's is meant to be a book about culture and imperialism and resistance! Likewise, no mention of Fanny Colonna's study of Algerian schoolmasters under colonialism, which describes so well how the Algerians had to wend their way between traditional, Reformed and French educational systems: a book which really lays bare the realities of living between a set of cultures, one old, one self-transforming and one alien. The disregard of the concrete realities of Algeria, the barely restrained indulgence in a kind of metaphysical projection of an abstract theme, would make it difficult to defend Said against the charge that he is indeed an Orientalist, in the negative sense he has himself bestowed on the term.

The most interesting of all French novels about North Africa (which, as it happens, conflates Morocco and Algeria), Montherlant's *La Rose de Sable*, is similarly unmentioned. It should have been a kind of 'Passage to Algeria', but for the fact that Montherlant did not publish it in the 1930s, when he had written it, claiming retrospectively that he did not wish to weaken France at a moment when war with Hitler was imminent. At the time, he only published a small part of it, dealing with a cross-cultural love-affair, publishing the rest only when the battle of decolonization was over. Yet he claimed that he had made no changes, so that the novel represents his true views as they were even before the battle was decided, and that this can be checked by consulting the original manuscript in the appropriate Paris library. As Montherlant was not famous for truthfulness, I had always hoped that someone would indeed check this, and who more qualified than an anti-Orientalist? The love-affair in *La Rose de Sable* is moving (though marred by the implausible assumption that it is possible to have a liaison in an oasis without the entire oasis knowing of it), and differs from Gide's activities in Biskra not only by being heterosexual, but by liberating the hero, not from puritanism, but from colonialism. So why is it missing from *Culture and Imperialism*? Both its contents, the circumstances of its publication and non-publication, and possible changes in its content in the wake of shifts in political climate, could hardly be more relevant to Said's theme.

Personally, I regret, most of all, the absence of those great summits of French anthropology in the Maghreb, Emile Masqueray and Robert Montagne. The ideas of the former (the man himself is, unjustly, forgotten) live on through Durkheim and Evans-Pritchard and have enhanced our understanding of human society. Is that to be castigated as Orientalism? The latter is particularly interesting from the viewpoint of Said's problem. Montagne was unquestionably a colonialist, a naval officer who entered scholarship through military (ethnographic) intelligence. What he said about the Berbers was that they both were, and were not, like 'us' Europeans: notwithstanding obvious superficial features, their society does not resemble our Middle Ages, but it does resemble the ancient Greeks. Most Europeans, I suspect, are more proud of the *polis* than of the baron's keep, as their institutional ancestor. Was Montagne guilty of Orientalism? I happen to think he just got it right.

Said writes well, though not always lucidly, and his comments on the involvement of literature with society are interesting. His heart is in the right place at least when he urges us not to freeze people in their social categories. In the end, we are all human. But the central undercurrent of his work is that some of us are, in virtue of our historic position, condemned to travesty others: 'culture played a very important, indeed an *indispensable* role. At the heart of European culture during the many decades of imperial expansion lay an undeterred and unrelenting Eurocentrism' (emphasis mine). Was this so? Montagne was a colonialist, but he got it right. Fanon was an anti-colonialist, but was closer to metaphysics than to the peasantry. Gide was a critic of colonialism, but his Algeria is simply an erotic fantasy. Sartre was anti-colonialist, but was brazenly willing to suppress the truth about gulags so as to protect his darling French working class from emotional discomfort. Truth is not linked to political virtue (either directly or inversely). To insinuate the opposite is to be guilty of that very sin which Said wishes to denounce. Like the rain, truth falls on both the just and the unjust. The problem of power and culture, and their turbulent relations during the great metamorphosis of our social world, is too important to be left to lit crit.

13

From the Ruins
of the Great Contest:
Civil Society, Nationalism
and Islam

The events which occurred, significantly, around the 200th anniversary of the French Revolution, have not merely changed the political map of Europe. They have also radically transformed our conceptual map of the options facing human society. It is as well to go briefly over the historical background to all this.

As it emerged from the Middle Ages, Europe came to be divided into two halves by the Reformation and the Counter-Reformation. In its north-west corner, societies emerged which gradually moved towards limited and accountable government, a raising of the status accorded to commerce and production in comparison with inherited status, martial honour and political domination, and a generalized individualism and freedom of thought. By the eighteenth century, this new world was visibly outdistancing its southern rival not only in wealth but also, ironically, in the very field in which its rival claimed to excel, namely warfare. The Dutch had beaten the powerful Iberian monarchy, and the English nation of shopkeepers had repeatedly beaten the larger French nation of military aristocrats. This, in conjunction with the unprecedented growth of science and technology, which eventually enabled the new commercial nations to complete the transition from predation to production, provided food for deep reflection: though the term was not then in use, the *ancien régime* was the first case of self-conscious and self-deploring under-development. The sustained attempt to understand and remedy this condition was known as the Enlightenment.

Its message was that tyranny and superstition were not neces-sary features of the human condition, but rather a kind of avoid-able mistake. They could be replaced by a more benign order based on liberty and truth. The financial *Krach* of the French monarchy made it possible to try and implement this idea. It turned out not to work at the first try, leading first to a Terror, and then a new dictatorship. This in turn stimulated further reflection concerning what had gone wrong.

The most famous among the fruits of this reflection was Marxism. The basic idea is simple: it is useless to try to impose the rule of Reason and Nature by simple fiat, or by the imple-mentation of a design. One must first of all know the nature of the material with which one is working, i.e. human society. One must understand the laws of its transformation. Marxism claimed to possess such understanding. In the meantime, commercializa-tion had led to a brutally inegalitarian and atomized society, and the Marxist critique also promised to remedy the blatant moral defects of this latest social type, intended by history as the penul-timate form of human co-operation, the curtain-raiser to final salvation.

By the twentieth century, the earlier bifurcation of Europe, which had been engendered, or perhaps ratified, by the Reforma-tion, was eventually overcome, by the belated industrialization of southern Europe. But after 1917 and 1945, a new bifurcation emerged. The division now was East–West rather than North–South. It separated a Europe based on an ambiguous post-Reformation compromise, with many elements drawn from the Enlightenment, but lacking much ideological coherence and unification, from an ideocratic Eastern Europe, committed to the sustained and uncompromising imposition of the Marx-revised Enlightenment vision. The two halves of Europe presented two rival ways of seeing the world and of running society.

For a considerable time, the outcome of the Great Contest, as

Isaac Deutscher christened it (though he had been anticipated by John Stuart Mill), was far from obvious. Given the appalling devastation wrought by two world wars, a civil war and a brutal collectivization, not to mention purges, the achievement of turning Russia into a superpower, a world co-sovereign, with a literate and industrial population, and capable for a time of actually taking the lead in space exploration, was impressive. If the Soviet Union went on like this, it looked as if it might well win. For a time it seemed as if Marxism might be a secular version of Calvinism, an austere determinism, which would do for collective, deliberate and emulative industrialization what the original version was said to have done for the unintended first emergence of an individualist modernity. It would provide that moral fibre, which alone would make it possible to round the cape, and weather its storms. If, in the course of all this, it was somewhat inimical to liberty, that was a price worth paying. One can hardly pass through a great storm without severe discipline. Inside the faith, it wasn't possible to use this argument in so many words, which would turn the vision itself into an instrument of the historical Cunning of Reason; but something not too far removed from it can be found among the works of some of the theoreticians of the regime.

But no one in the end gave much credence to this, because the historic achievement, which such a theory would explain and justify, did not in the end materialize. Quite the reverse. After the initial great successes of winning the war and securing a first in space, the Soviet system became humanly less horrible, but at the same time visibly second-rate in effectiveness. Terror was replaced by squalor. The *nomenklatura* ceased shooting each other and began bribing each other instead. Dissidents were sentenced to long prison-terms, not shot out of hand. By the late 1980s, it was all over. The identity of the victor in the Great Contest had become blatantly obvious, above all, to many members of the leading stratum of a vanquished society.

It is true that virtually all sovietologists had agreed that the system could not possibly reform itself: any serious attempt to do so would be disastrous for the power and position of the enormous dominant *apparat*, which could not and would not cut its own throat. These pessimists may yet be proved right, to the extent that the system is indeed incapable of reforming itself without collapsing, which it may be in the process of doing. It is enormously to the credit of the *apparat*, or at any rate important segments of it, that, although the liberal trend must have seemed so self-evidently disastrous to many of them, there has been so little by way of determined attempts to suppress it. The New Class, so often and so plausibly accused of being good for and at nothing other than maintaining its own power, has suddenly developed a remarkable squeamishness in pursuing its single aim. It has presided over a political disintegration, hardly paralleled in any country which had not first undergone military defeat. One inept attempted coup, whose failure presumably sprang at least in part from the inner vacillation of some of its leaders, and acts of political violence in Tbilisi, the Baltic and elsewhere – these are indeed deplorable, but astonishingly mild stuff compared with what this part of the world was used to in the days when every-one knew that politics is about who does whom. So far, the astonishing thing about the disintegration of the Soviet empire is not how much, but how little violence has accompanied it. All this may, of course, still change.

What now? The central new idea and ideal which emerged in the run-up to liberalization was that of 'Civil Society'. In prac-tice, this notion has a number of components. One of them is the end of ideocracy, of secular messianism, of a society based on obligatory Truth. This was part of Marxism's heritage from the Enlightenment: if oppression had been based on superstition, then a free society would be based on truth. This time, it would be revealed by Nature, rather than from beyond Nature. In fact, civil society is based on the denial of ideological monopoly, on the acceptance of compromise on deep issues concerning the nature of things, on doubt, irony and all kinds of adjustments. Men are allowed to have fundamental beliefs, though these may no longer serve as premises for their social arrangements, but be held partly in suspension, when men meet in the assembly and the market. Of course, we cannot act in a vacuum and all collective action has some kind of background set of assumptions, but these are now fairly incoherent, unsystematic, negotiated and unstable. So the *ancien régime*, based on False Faith, is not replaced by a true Faith, not even one (as in the Marxist version) reinforced by a plausible historical sociology. It is replaced by doubt and a separation of private from public conviction. George Orwell was wrong when he ascribed 'doublethink' to totalitarianism. In another, but still relevant sense, the mastery of doublethink is also essential for liberals, and those who manage liberal societies. They cannot be wholly without beliefs, but they must also know when and how to suspend them, and co-operate with those who hold rival ones. The recognition of this need is one way in which our map of human society has changed.

The collapse of Marxist societies was in effect the collapse of a moral order. This had been the first secular *Umma* or sacramental community, based on a doctrine of total salvation, articulated in a naturalistic and sociological idiom rather than a transcendental one. But it *was* a moral order: the background belief accounted for everything and allocated a place to everything, it covered Morals as well as Faith, it endorsed the state and was endorsed by it. It had its own theodicy, it explained evil, thus turning it into necessary evil, and it guaranteed that in due course evil would be overcome.

For a long time, many of those who lived within the walls of the Soviet state also consented to live within its conceptual walls, at least in broad outline, even if they had doubts about the detail. The period of stagnation had quietly eroded this acceptance, and *perestroika* merely enabled everyone to say out loud what they had privately come to suspect, namely that the Emperor was naked. But in the West, when the death of God was announced, it was done in a society which had long prepared itself, intellectually and institutionally, for such a demise, and another vision, not so comforting perhaps or fully rounded, but none the less viable, was available, ready for use. The death of the Marxist God-surrogate may raise graver problems. Dostoevski worried whether man could live without God. His successors must wonder whether he can live without historical materialism. The collapse of the first-ever secular faith, or at any rate the first to become a state religion, came with brutal suddenness, without any alternative being agreed or ready for deployment. This suddenness, and the unavailability of a credible alternative, was as marked in the sphere of ideology as in that of the polity.

The emergence of a new compromise, and the rules governing its implementation, took a long time to mature in the West. It seems to have arisen out of a truce between the ritualistic priests of superstition and the enthusiast–puritans. The compromise was worked out against a background of prosperity, and the effective functioning of that other element of a civil society, a safe and autonomous productive zone. The establishment of similar compromise on the territories of the erstwhile Soviet Union has to be attempted without any of these advantages, but on the contrary, against the background of a collapsing economy and a pulverized civil society.

What the Russians and the other members of the new Union are attempting is, all at once, to dismantle an empire, to operate an economic miracle, to transform a moral and economic climate, to turn a gulag state into a nightwatchman, to settle old national border and other disputes, and to revive a culture. If any significant part of this agenda is achieved, we shall indeed be able, and obliged, to salute a miracle.

The Great Contest was in part about whether there was indeed a messianic, naturalistic counter-truth, which would replace the old absolutism of kings and priests, or whether the new order would have to make do with compromise and muddle. But, though this may have been the deepest, it was not the most conspicuous issue separating the Great Contestants: which was whether resources should be controlled and owned individually or collectively. The two issues are, however, intimately connected. A genuine absolutist ideocracy must be socialist; and a genuine, full-blooded socialism must also be an absolutist ideocracy. That much has now become evident, and is part of the new map of society. This does not mean that a moderate or compromise socialism (a mixed economy, a powerful public sector, overall political control over limits of market freedom, an effective welfare state) must lead to absolutism: far from it. It does, however, mean that if, on the basis of the idea that private control and the 'classes' it engenders are the root of all social evil, all productive resources are brought under social (hence central, because modern society cannot be segmentary) control, then there simply is no base for effective opposition to the central machinery of the state. Political centralization is inherent in a complex division of labour, and if full economic centralization is added to it, nothing remains to counter-balance the central *apparat*. A modern society cannot delegate coercion and the maintenance of order to sub-units, for it cannot live with the institutionalized feud; therefore, the only way it can diffuse power is by doing so in the economic sphere, and making economic rights reasonably sacrosanct. Conversely, no society which is truly absolutist can preserve a fully independent economy: in economic life, rival centres exist, ready to take over when the state allows them to do so. This is why right-wing dictatorships find it so much easier to liberalize than leftist ones: they have a proto-civil society waiting in the wings.

The society which is being dismantled in the former Soviet Union was absolutist, ideocratic and socialist, features which were inherently linked. It is not surprising that the transition to the market is proving so difficult. Apart from competent operators, the market 'only' needs the Nightwatchman state, but it does need it. At the very moment when the market is being established, in an area in any case not over-endowed with the appropriate human and cultural material, that state, which should succour and protect it, is disintegrating. It was based on fear and the pretence of unanimity, and both are gone. There is no formula for transforming the monolithic and all-embracing state into a minimal one. It has never been tried before, and, as far as I know, no one has tried to work out a theory of how it could be done (largely because, until it was actually attempted, no one believed it would ever be tried. So no theory was really required, for mankind, as Marx did not quite say, does not bother to solve problems which have not yet arisen).

These, then, are the two main and linked problems: the establishment of an ideological compromise sufficient to make the system work yet not strong enough to stifle enterprise, and like-wise, of a political order capable of maintaining order and pro-tecting a fragile new economy, yet not throttling it. These things generally take time; the Russians, having had to endure the imposition from above of a blueprint for a supposedly perfect social order, must, in the course of dismantling it, resolve the paradox of how to establish, once again, more or less from above, an uncentralized pluralism. It doesn't seem to be going too well. It has to be done this way, for there is no time to wait for a more gentle maturation. A society-by-design has left a dreadful herit-age to its successor: it too must be created by design and quickly established, even if the faith sustaining such a procedure has now gone. This time, it is the logic of the situation, and not doctrine, which requires it.

This problem is being faced against the background of an-other: that of nationalism. A modern society is a mass, anony-mous one in which work is semantic not physical, and in which men can only claim effective economic and political citizenship if they can operate the language and culture of the bureaucracies which surround them. The socio-economic processes which helped establish a liberal consumerist society in the West also engen-dered nationalism, for men can now only live comfortably in pol-itical units dedicated to the maintenance of the same culture as their own. So in the West, the emergence of modernity was ac-companied by the emergence of nationalism. During the first half of our century, it even looked as if nationalism might become the dominant partner, and would transform industrial society in its own image. The outcome of the Second World War happily eliminated that option.

In the course of the 70 (or in some regions, 40) years of its existence, the Bolshevik ideocracy did not have too much trouble in restraining nationalism, any more than the relatively mild *ancien régime* in Eastern and Central-eastern Europe did in containing it between 1815 and 1918. But the collapse of the communist empire in 1989 and thereafter left few obstacles in the way of free nationalist expression – other than that of rival nationalisms. The phenomenon of nationalism is like a recurring decimal, it has no end, every national flea has smaller fleas to plague it in turn, not to mention the fact that fleas of the same size also torment each other.

The striking parallels between the collapse of the Bolshevik empire and the Habsburg one are frightening. Generally speaking, the successor states are smaller, less experienced and generally weaker, but endowed with every disadvantage of the previous imperial unit – they are haunted by additional minorities, including members of the erstwhile dominant culture, which are unused to their new subordinate status, and endowed with cultural cousins who may help them resist it when the time comes.

The newly emerging order is having to cope with nationalism under conditions which are both worse and better than those which prevailed in similar situations earlier. Bolshevism had destroyed civil society, or very nearly: there were few institutions other than those which were parts of the central *apparat*. As I have said, nothing much was waiting in the wings when the one unique actor on the political scene collapsed. But nationalism can be activated very quickly. It is based on the eagerness with which we identify with those of the same culture as ourselves, and sustained by the crucial new role of culture as the marker of collective boundaries, rather than of individual status, which is what culture used to be. Events have shown this to be so (assuming it had ever been in doubt). The need for pluralism, only dubiously satisfied by other new candidates, has been only too effectively met by the emergence of national movements.

Modern nationalism, which is a passionate identification with large, anonymous communities of shared culture and cultural imagery, creates its units out of pre-existing differences of various kinds. Among these, religious ones are important (irrespective of whether the faith which defined the religions in question is still upheld), as the Yugoslav conflict between groups of similar speech and ancestry, but diverse religion, illustrates.

A very significant part of the erstwhile Soviet empire is Muslim. Islam has a very distinctive place among the world religions. At least so far, it seems uniquely resistant to secularization. One might say that whereas the Marxists have totally lost their faith but developed a strong craving for civil society, the Muslims have retained and even strengthened their faith, but accommodate themselves without too much reluctance to clientelist, cynical politics. They do not seem to miss civil society too much. In the Muslim areas, the balance of clientelism and nationalism seems more tilted towards the former than is the case in non-Muslim zones. During the quasi-democratic sunset of the Soviet Union, before it finally gave up the ghost, the manipulability of Muslim votes by its patron-brokers was a standing joke.

The mechanisms which underlie Muslim fundamentalism, of an identification with an anonymous *Umma*, are similar to those which underlie modern nationalism: men leaving, or deprived of places in a local social structure, are attracted by identification with a community defined by a shared High Culture. Muslims brought into a newly centralized polity and economy abandon the old local shrine, which had served communities that no longer exist, and ratify, through adherence to a scripturalist version of the faith, both their ascension from the backwoods, and their loyalty to their co-religionists and opposition to outsiders. They also find in the faith a kind of prefabricated Constitutional Law, which sits in judgement on their own rulers, and obliges them at least to enforce the Law, even if not to refrain from mafioso-style politics. How all this will operate in the Union of Sovereign States remains to be seen, but it is bound to make its distinctive contribution.

Never before has state-building proceeded under such complex, and probably such difficult, circumstances. Marxism had taught that civil society was a kind of moral fraud, but 70 years of secular messianism has engendered a passionate thirst for just this fraud. Marxism had seen the liberal state as a kind of executive committee of the bourgeoisie: now a committee is striving, not too convincingly, to create a bourgeoisie which it could serve, and hopes that it is not too blatant a lumpenbourgeoisie. We can only watch these efforts with trepidation, and wish them well. The best one can say is that a dogmatic pessimism is unjustified.

So, at this moment, Atlantic civilization, itself committed to consumerism, pluralism and aversion to ideological enthusiasm, is endowed with two rather remarkable contrasted neighbours on its Eastern and South-eastern borders: one, totally abandoning its erstwhile all-absorbing faith, but pervaded by a strong yearning for civil society, and the other, strong and unwavering in its reformed Faith, but with only feeble strivings for pluralism and accountable government, and on the contrary, accommodating itself without too much protest to clientelist and rapacious politics. This combination of fundamentalist moralism in social life with cynicism in politics strikes outsiders as hypocritical, but it has a certain logic and coherence: rulers are expected to enforce, or, at least, not to violate the Law, but otherwise they arouse no very high expectations.

The Gulf War offered a foretaste of the type of international order this situation may engender. There is a kind of Consumerist International of developed or semi-developed societies, united in placing production over coercion or 'honour', or, at any rate, seeking power through production rather than force, and having both dissociated glory from territory, and abjured faith in a unique and obligatory salvation, no longer inclined to go to war against each other. On the contrary, they have a shared interest in the maintenance of peace and order. But they share the planet with other regions, in which there are societies which exemplify either the rule of honour-oriented coercers, or which take an absolutist Faith seriously and literally, or both of these conditions at once.

It seems fairly obvious that the curve of development is pointing in a direction where very terrible weapons of diverse kinds will be increasingly cheap, easy to acquire and to deploy. If one combines this premise with the recognition of the continued existence of societies either committed to doctrinal absolutism, or governed by men who have come up through inter-mafia struggles and know nothing else, the conclusion is inevitable: sooner or later, either some intellectually limited thugs, or some uncompromising believers (or possibly someone who combines traits of both these characters), will be in possession or means through which they can effectively blackmail the world.

The Consumerist Unbeliever International has every interest in ganging up with each other to prevent this from taking place. At the time of the Gulf War, this did indeed seem to be happening, but as far as I know, no one spelt it out, and no attempt was made to institutionalize it all and create a case law which would prevent a repetition of the crisis. Maybe things will have to get much worse before the intellectual clarity and political will emerge which will bring this about.

In the past, the political fragmentation of mankind has been a great blessing: the multi-state system ensured that the whole of mankind did not ever make the same mistake at the same time. The ecological problem, and the consequences of the development of military technology, may oblige mankind in the future to abandon this 'insurance through political diversification'. Perhaps one can reach a point of least evil by combining world government by the Consumerist Unbeliever International, with the maintenance of the maximum possible cultural independence of the constituent units.

14

An Alternative Vision

The stages of nationalism proposed (see chapter 2) differ from those offered in the powerfully argued, well documented and influential work of Miroslav Hroch.[1] As Eric Hobsbawm observes[2] 'the work of Hroch . . . opened the new era in the analysis of the composition of national liberation movements.' Hroch, in the work cited, represents an interesting attempt to save *both* Marxism, and the nationalist vision of itself, and this constitutes part of its interest: nations really do exist, on this view, and express themselves through nationalist striving, instead of being, as I argue, engendered by it, and being its creation. At the same time, the transition between the postulated Marxist modes of production does remain for Hroch *the* basic event of the age, and the (autonomous?) nationalist development is plotted against that event. It takes its character from the manner in which the two processes coalesce. Hroch's outstandingly well-documented argument deserves full examination, though I disagree with him on both counts: nations do not 'really exist' (they only emerge as a special form of correlation of culture and polity, under certain

---

[1] Hroch, Miroslav, *Social Preconditions of National Revival in Europe*. Cambridge University Press, Cambridge, 1985.
[2] Hobsbawm, Eric, *Nations and Nationalism since 1780*. Cambridge University Press, Cambridge, 1990, p. 4.

far from universal economic conditions); and the Marxist thesis of the feudalism/capitalism transition is acceptable only if reinterpreted as the transition from the agrarian to the industrial world.

So Hroch's typology or periodicization is engendered by the superimposition of two sets of distinctions. One of them is defined in terms of the two allegedly crucial stages of the overall social order; the other, in terms of the successive character of the national movement itself. The first distinction is binary: it refers to the distinction between feudalism and absolutism on the one hand, and capitalism on the other. The book was written from an avowedly Marxist viewpoint, though at the time it was written and published, it could hardly have seen the light of day in Prague had it been formulated in any other way. This does not necessarily imply that the Marxism of the argument was less than sincere: that is a question which it would seem to be inappropriate to raise here. At the same time, this is obviously a part of the background of the book, and it cannot be ignored.

The use of the Marxist theory of historical stages calls for some comments. Hroch, as stated, combines 'feudalism' and 'absolutism' into *one* 'stage'.[3] It is no doubt perfectly possible to include both of them with a broader, generic 'feudalism': within each of them status is linked to land. Within each, there is a sharply differentiated system of ranks, connected with unsymmetrical obligations and duties, and organized in a pyramid, with a monarchical apex. In each, there is an ethos of martial valour, a low valuation of productive work, and an ever lower or ambiguous valuation of commerce and trade. The terminology of rank under centralized absolutism is the same as in, and is inherited from, feudalism in the narrower sense. So they do share certain important features.

But the differences are at least as great and as important as the similarities. An absolutist state relies largely on a standing and

---

[3]   Hroch, *Social Preconditions*, pp. 10, 25. For instance, on p. 25 he refers to 'the period when the decisive feature of social conflict was the struggle against feudalism and absolutism'.

professional army, within which the nobility may serve as officers, but to which they do not normally bring their own entire social units 'in arms'. The 'regiment' of a given nobleman, or one named after him, is in fact a standard unit subject to regularized rules of equipment and retinue in arms, re-organized for a campaign, and run in terms of its own local, particularist traditions. The absolutist monarch controls the territory over which he is sovereign, and legal and political authority in outlying or inaccessible regions is not delegated to nobles with a local powerbase. (As Adam Smith noted in connection with Cameron of Lochiel, such delegation, unsanctioned by law, did in fact occur in the pre-1745 Highlands, but it was just this which made the Highlands so scandalously untypical, and exceptional in an otherwise centralized state.)[4] Under absolutism, the *noblesse d'épée* is complemented and in some measure replaced by a *noblesse de robe* – in effect, a bureaucracy. With the Tudors, for instance, a new nobility with a service ethos complemented and replaced an independent, territorially based aristocracy. Benjamin Constant stresses this general point in his essay on F. Schiller's *Wallenstein*. Wallenstein's army was a collection of gangs, bound only by personal loyalty to a successful military chief – quite unlike the orderly, bureaucratized armies established by the eighteenth and nineteenth centuries, and not comparable with them. It was the Protestant Dutch who invented and codified a standard set of military movements and words of command, which characterize a modern army. Rationalization on the battlefield and drill square is as important as it is in the work-place.

It is significant that the name Tocqueville does not occur in Hroch's bibliography. The idea that the French Revolution completed, rather than reversed, the work of the centralizing French monarch, receives no discussion. The French Revolution is in fact only mentioned once (though the generic notion of 'bourgeois revolution' occurs far more frequently and plays an important role in the argument). When the French Revolution is mentioned by name, it occurs in the context of methodological

[4]   Smith, Adam, *The Wealth of Nations*.

discussion, and of an affirmation of the author's then commitment to a Marxist view of history, and to seeing *class*, rather than so to speak surface social position, as ultimately significant.[5]

It is tempting to suggest that at this point at least, this author's indisputably most important argument, suffers not from an excess, but from a lack of Marxism. Marxism distinguishes *various* types of class-endowed society, it is we post-Marxist sociologists who bring together all agrarian societies in one great genus, contrasted with the industrial world. The assumption of a generic (and homogeneous?) social baseline, a catch-all feudalism–absolutism, prevents him from even raising the question of the relation of the rise of nationalism to *earlier* structural changes in European society. But it clearly is, at the very least, necessary to ask the question concerning the relation of nationalism to that earlier transition, which led from a politically fragmented genuinely feudal society, within which bureaucracy was largely absent, or at best present in, or drawn from, the Church, to that later 'absolutist' society, in which a secular bureaucracy is already prominent.[6] In that later social order, widespread administrative use of writing already begins to engender that linkage of a centralized polity and a literate, normative, codified High Culture, which lies close to the essence of the nationalist principle. Nationalist movements did not yet emerge in this period, but it is probable that it prepared the ground for them, through the centralization, bureaucratization and standardization which it practised.[7] Whether or not this is so, one should at least be able to ask the question. Hroch's stark binary opposition makes it hard to do so. Though, on the whole, I subscribe to the view that nationalism, in the form in which we know it, is a phenomenon of the last two centuries, nevertheless it must be a defect of a theory of nationalism if, by starting so uncompromisingly from

[5]   *Social Preconditions*, p. 17.

[6]   Anderson, Perry, *The Lineages of the Absolute State*.

[7]   Mann, Michael, 'The emergence of modern European nationalism', in J. Hall and I. Jarvie (eds), *Transition to Modernity*, Cambridge University Press, Cambridge, 1992.

an implicitly generic baseline of 'absolutism–feudalism', it inhibits the formulation of questions concerning possible earlier roots.

There are other candidates for this role of early progenitors or harbingers of nationalism, notably the Reformation and, to a lesser extent perhaps, the Renaissance. The Protestant use of vernacular languages and the diffusion of literacy, and the direct contact of the believer with the Sacred Word (in an idiom intelligible to him) clearly has affinity with the social profile of nationalism. Whether communication with the deity or the bureaucracy is involved, either way, frequent and unmediated contact calls for a standardized and intelligible code. Regular verbal intercourse with either deity or official, helps the formulation of a shared, 'national' culture. The creation of national rather than international clergies, or the diffusion of the clergy status throughout the whole of society, the abolition of privileged access and idiom, cannot be irrelevant to the eventual emergence of the nationalist ideal of one culture, one state, one society. Protestant elimination of esotericism in religion has a great affinity with nationalist proscription of culturally marked differences of social status. The fragmentation of the universal political system, the diffusion of sovereignty, also cannot but be a significant part of the prehistory, if not the history, of nationalism. When Bernard Shaw causes his version of St Joan to be burnt as a Protestant by the Church and as a nationalist by the English, was he being altogether anachronistic? The absence of the name of Jan Hus from the index of a Czech book on nationalism is also strange. The theological rather than ethnographic orientation of this proto-nationalism would not have fitted Hroch's theme. Jan Hus codified the Czech language but he was not an ethnographer.

So one can only repeat the point that, in a curious way, this remarkable work in part suffers not from an excess, but an insufficiency of Marxism. The major social transition to which its argument links nationalism is simply the move from absolutism–feudalism to industrialization, and it altogether ignores earlier, and possibly relevant, transitions. A person like the present writer, who does believe that nationalism is indeed essentially linked to the coming of industrialism, cannot wholly disagree with such an approach, and does not greatly object to the use of 'capital-ism' where 'industrialism' would be more appropriate: that is simply a part of the Marxist idiom, and was made mandatory by the repudiation of the convergence-of-capitalist-and-socialist-industrialism thesis, to which Marxist regimes were committed, and one can easily carry out one's own translation of the termi-nology here. Nevertheless, one feels that the convention that the world began in the late eighteenth century, for which I feel some sympathy, is carried to excess in this argument.

In this connection, it is of course also worth noting that the discussion of the implications for nationalism of the anticipated later transition from capitalism to *socialism* is equally absent. Its handling would of course have been extremely delicate. Work attempting to handle the role of ethnicity in Soviet Society (that of the late Yulian Bromley) is however cited. The emergence of nationalism is traced up to its fusion with mass political agita-tion: the crucial issue of its subsequent fate is ignored – as was its pre-history.

The basic logic of Hroch's approach then is to relate nation-alism to a single and stark transition, namely that from pre-industrial to capitalist society. What exactly is it that is then brought into relation with the underlying single great change in social ecology and structure?

The answer is – the phenomenology of nationalism. Here Hroch operates no longer with a binary, but a three-term classification, a three-stage account of the development of nationalism. Hroch distinguishes between stage A, that of scholarly interest in and exploration of the culture of a nation, stage B, of nationalist agitation – the intellectuals no longer restrict themselves to eth-nography, but promote national awareness amongst the popula-tion whose national culture they investigate – and finally stage C, the emergence of a mass national movement.

This typology is inspired by and is specially applicable to (as the author recognizes) the emergence of 'small' nations not al-ready endowed with, so to speak, their own and distinctive po-litical roof. So, by implication – though the author does not formulate it in any way – the two dimensions which are formally introduced (traditional/capitalist, and the three stages of national awakening), are *also* related to a third dimension, constituted by the distinction between large and state-endowed nations, and small, 'oppressed' ones. In this dichotomy, state-endowment would seem to be more important than the size in a literal sense, in as far as Danes appear to be consigned to the 'large nation', which can hardly be correct in some simple numerical sense.[8] It turns the Danes into a large nation, and the Ukrainians, a small one.

Formally speaking, this dimension or variable does not enter the argument, in as far as the official, formally announced subject of Hroch's inquiry is indeed the nationalism of 'small' nations only, i.e. nations which need to *acquire* their political unit, their High Culture and their ruling class. 'Large' nations are excluded only from the term of reference and so, officially, not discussed. However, this focus on small, 'oppressed' nations, nevertheless implies a more general theory which would treat them as one, distinctive variety of nation-formation. So a wider typology is implied, which would cover both species, the 'great' and 'small' alike.

However, officially at least, at the heart of the book there is only the relationship between the two-fold classification of societies, and the three-fold classification of stages of nationalism. The manner in which these two overlap with each other then leads Hroch to propose four types of nationalism.[9]

The first type he calls the 'integrated type' of development. The transition from scholarly interest to active agitation precedes the industrial and bourgeois revolutions. The completion of the 'formation of a modern nation' follows these, and is in turn followed by the emergence of a working-class movement. The Czechs would be an example.

The second species he calls the 'belated type': national agitators replace scholars before the coming of the bourgeois and industrial revolutions, but the emergence of a working-class movement

---

[8]   *Social Preconditions*, p. 8.
[9]   *Social Preconditions*, p. 27 et seq.

precedes or is contemporaneous with the transition from agitation to mass nationalism, and the formation of a full modern
nation only follows all the other processes considered. The Slovaks
constitute a specimen of this type.

The third variety he calls the 'insurrectional type': agitators
replace scholars already under feudal society, and a modern nation
is actually formed under feudalism: 'The national movement had
already attained a mass character under the conditions of feudal
society.' The nation is formed before the emergence of bourgeois
society.[10] This is the Balkan situation. In conversation, Hroch
has stressed that this type presents a major problem for my linkage of nationalism with industrialization, which indeed it does.

Finally, there is the fourth species, which he calls 'disinte-
grated': in this variety, even the early forms of nationalist activity
only follow the bourgeois and industrial revolutions, and the
nationalist agitation is not necessarily replaced by a mass movement at all. The generalization which seems to follow (and the
author articulates it, though not quite in these words) is that very
early industrialization can be fatal for nationalism. Cultures which
pass through industrialization without constituting boundaries of
a disadvantaged class or region, would seem to have no political
future – unless they *already* had their state, even before transition. Some of the late and ineffective Western European nationalisms seem to be what he has in mind.

An interesting and distinctive aspect of Hroch's approach is
the importance of phase A in nation-forming, which he describes
as follows: 'The beginning of every national revival is marked by
a passionate concern on the part of a group of individuals, usually intellectuals, for the study of the language, the culture, the
history of the oppressed nationalist.'[11] Hroch rightly notes that
quite often these ethnic explorers are not members of the ethnic

---

[10]   The author's European orientation seems to prevent him from considering
       the parallel case of nationalist sentiment in societies which are partially
       feudal, but still have significant tribal traits – e.g. Somalis, Kurds, possibly
       some ethnic groups on the territory of the USSR.
[11]   *Social Preconditions*, p. 22.

group in question: the awakening does not necessarily or exclusively come, so to speak, from *within*. There often are vicarious Awakeners.

The presence and salience of this situation could usefully be made into a *variable* in a general theory of nationalism, which would embrace 'large' and 'small' nations alike, rather than being, as it is in Hroch's argument, a *constant* in the study of small nations (by which Hroch as stated means not size, but the initial absence of an indigenous ruling class, High Culture and state). If we adopt such an approach, we can both see that, and *why*, this stage is so prominent in some of the European time zones, and absent in others. (See chapter 2, on E. H. Carr, for a definition of the zones.) In the Westernmost time zone, national unity is forged not with, but against the peasantry. 'Peasant' is a term of abuse, not of endearment, in such societies.[12] National unity and the sense of nationhood is formed in a 'Jacobin' spirit, around an already existing and expanding set of central institutions, and the High Culture associated with it. Peasant regional idiosyncrasy is an offensive hindrance, and it is to be ironed out as quickly as possible, by an educational system which holds this to be one of its most important objectives. In the second time zone, populist romanticism *is* encountered, especially in Germany: the fragmented political units, preceding national unification, often practised alien speech and manners in their courts, and so the local culture is stressed in opposition to this alien style. None the less, a sense of national unity is forged against and not in support of regional dialects and lifestyles, and ethnography is not the handmaiden of nationalism. When Mussolini encouraged Italians from the South and from Veneto to settle in the Val d'Aosta, he was, all at once, combating both the good French speech of the Savoyard ruling class, habituated to seek

[12]   In Angus Wilson's insightful novel about historians, *Anglo-Saxon Attitudes*, there is a perceptive account of the incomprehension occurring between two middle-class women, one French, the other Scandinavian. For the Frenchwoman, peasant is a pejorative notion, and she simply cannot grasp the admiring, nostalgic, romantic–populist use of the idea by the other lady.

their brides in Chambéry rather than in Italy, *and* the idiosyncratic local dialect of the Valdotain peasantry.

It is in the third time zone that this ethnographic 'phase' is pervasively and inherently present. Here, a national and state culture is created not in opposition to peasant idiosyncrasy, but on the basis of it. A Folk Culture is used to forge an operational High Culture. Of course, this culture has to be sifted and distilled and standardized; but none the less, it must first of all be investigated in its raw state, if it is ever to be streamlined and codified, so as to provide the base for a new High Culture around which a nation and state are to be created. The much-used distinction between historic and non-historic nations matters relatively little: it does not make too much difference whether the dialect-group in question had, long ago, been linked to a political unit and its own court culture, or whether it had never had such a standing. It only makes a difference to the *content* of national myth which is to be created: the Czechs or Lithuanians can look back to medieval glories, whereas the Estonians, Belorussians or Slovaks cannot. Only peasant folklore or the odd social bandit, but no monarchs or imperial exploits, can enter their mythology. It looks as if there may be an amusing dispute between two post-communist states, Lithuania and Belarus, as to exactly which one is the legitimate heir of the glories of the medieval state normally referred to as Lithuania, but where, Belorussians claim, *their* language predominated.

The fourth or Soviet time zone of Europe possesses features both of the second and the third zones. Ethnic exploration, in the form of slavophil populism, not only existed but was extremely important and prominent. But its point was not so much to create a national identity as a basis for a new state: a state already existed, and was linked to a national Church, which seems to have done a good job in creating a national cultural identity. When *narodnost*, controversially, joined Orthodoxy and Autocracy in the triad of pillars of Czarism, did it mean ethnicity or rootedness? The celebrated 'going to the people' was concerned more with the definition or modification or re-establishment of the 'true content' of the national culture, than with its actual *creation.* Was this culture to be based on the values of peasant lifestyle and religiosity, or on the elite or courtly orientation, with its strong Westernizing tendency?

Amongst the other, non-Russian ethnic groups of the empire, on the other hand, the parallel with the third zone largely prevails. There is also the part of Europe which, in or around 1945, so to speak 'changed zones'. (In zone one, the Atlantic seaboard, state and culture were already linked. In zone two, Germany and Italy, a standardized normative *statsfähig* culture existed, but needed to find its political roots; in zone three, both national state and culture had to be created; and zone four resembled zone three, but the 'natural' development was distorted by 70 or 40 years of communism.)

One can sum up all this as follows: the nation-states which replaced dynastic–religious ones as the European norm in the two centuries following the French Revolution, could either grow around pre-existing states and/or High Cultures, or they could as it were roll their own culture out of existing folk traditions, and then form a state around such a newly created normative great tradition. In the latter case, a consciousness and memory had to be created, and ethnographic exploration (in effect: codification and invention) were mandatory. But in the former case, folk tradition, instead of having to be endowed with memory, had to be consigned to oblivion, and be granted, not the gift of memory, but of forgetfulness. The great theoretician of this path of nation-formation was of course Ernest Renan.[13] In the East they remember what never occurred, in the West they forget that which did occur. It was Renan who urged the French, in the interest of consistency, to abjure the political use of ethnography and ethnology: the boundaries of France never became ethnic, and they continue to invoke geopolitics and choice, rather than folk culture. So it was he who eloquently expounded the idea that the basis of national identity is not memory but amnesia: in the Jacobin French state, Frenchmen were induced to forget their

[13]   Renan, Ernest, *Qu'est-ce qu'une nation?* Paris, 1882. Republished in *Ernest Renan et l'Allemagne.* ed. E. Bure, New York, 1945.

origins, in contrast to the non-national Ottoman empire, where the very bases of social organization ensured that every man knew his ethnic–religious origin. To this day, Ottoman family legislation survives in Israel, thanks to a parliamentary balance which makes the religious vote valuable for most coalitions, and so helps ensure that a man can only marry in terms of his pre-modern, communal identity, by using its Church. So a pre-modern communal organization survives thanks to a parliamentary balance, engendered by proportional representation. Tradition can use modern voting methods to block modernity.

So ethnographic research is relevant in some but not all European contexts of nation-building: in others, its absence, or at least its political irrelevance, is just as important. Western nationalism ignores and does not explore folk diversity. So the options are – created memory, or induced oblivion. The great irony occurred in the history of social anthropology: through the enormously influential work of Bronislaw Malinowski, who virtually created and defined the British and Imperial school in this discipline, the kind of cultural–holist ethnography, initially practised in the interests of culture-preservation and nation-building in the East, was adapted in Western science in the name of and for the sake of empiricist method.[14] 'Going to the people' became, no longer a path to moral salvation or cultural preservation, but a tool of empiricist rigour against undisciplined speculation. Immersion in folk culture gives access to genuine social reality, whilst genetic–historical explanation is circular and speculative. Malinowski opposed both nationalist myths and the anthropology of Frazer. So a method invented as a pursuit of cultural and moral authenticity, is turned into a tool of empiricist science. Herder is made to serve Mach, and vice versa.

However, the main centre of Hroch's remarkable work lies not in his characteristically Central European stress on the contribution of ethnography to nation-building, but in his linking of the transformation of the European socio-economic system to the

---

[14]   Cf. *Malinowski Between Two Worlds*, eds R. Ellen, E. Gellner, G. Kubica, J. Mucha, Cambridge University Press, Cambridge, 1988.

rise of nationalism. Here, in effect, he faces one of the most persistent and deep issues in this field: is it nations, or is it classes, which are the real and principal actors in history? Or perhaps it is neither, or both? For him it is *both*.

He proclaims his intention to start from Marxist principles:

> We shall not disguise the fact that the generalising procedures we use in investigating hidden class and group interests and social relations are derived from the Marxist conception of historical development.[15]

Yet interestingly, his formal position also disavows any reductionism with respect to nations:

> In contrast with the subjectivist conception of the nation as the product of nationalism, the national will and spiritual forces, we posit the conception of the nation as a constituent of social reality of historical origin. We consider the origin of the modern nation as the fundamental reality and nationalism as a phenomenon derived from the existence of that nation.[16]

This affirmation could hardly be more clear or categorical. Nations or, strangely, 'the *origin* of the modern nation' (emphasis mine), is part of the basic social ontology, and not merely a historical by-product of structural change, although it seems (p. 4) that the characteristics which define a nation are not stable.

So his position in the book might be described as semi-Marxist: on the one hand, nations are granted an independent historical importance and reality, and are not reduced to a reflection of changes in class structure, and they remain at the centre of the stage. But the transition from feudalism/absolutism to capitalism *also* retains its central position. A discussion of the subsequent transition to socialism is largely avoided – which is understandable, though in an oblique way it remains present through the importance attributed to the emergence of a militant working-

---

[15]   Hroch, *Social Preconditions*, p. 17.
[16]   *Social Preconditions*, p. 3.

class movement, presumably meant to usher in a new era. It is neither affirmed nor denied that this working-class movement will eventually prevail and lead to new social formation altogether. There is nothing in the book to preclude anyone from supposing that this will indeed happen. Given the fact that the book was written and published under a regime which was formally committed to the view that it *had* already happened, and which did not permit any public denials of such a claim, the sheer fact it is not actually and explicitly affirmed, is not without interest.

So the overall conclusion of the book seems to be that, on the one hand, nations do have an independent and irreducible existence, and that none the less, the main historical reality remains the change in class relations postulated by Marxism. So the emergence of modern nations must be related to this great transformation – a task the book then carries out with an unrivalled empirical and conceptual thoroughness. Neither of the two great movements – the one on industrialism (or capitalism, in the book's terminology), the other to nationalism, is said to explain the other. The book conspicuously steers clear of any reductionism, either way: both Marxists and nationalists are granted their respective realms, and neither is allowed to claim domination over the other. By implication, the two realms are declared to be independent. This seems to me mistaken: in reality, both are aspects of *one single transition*.

But in the light of the actual more concrete findings of the book, can its conclusions really be sustained? Or is it the case that these admirable analyses and documentation in fact support quite a different view? Such a rival conclusion would, on the one hand, be far more reductionist *vis-à-vis* nations, and refrain from endorsing their ultimate reality; on the other hand, it would also take far less seriously the Marxist theory of social transition. It would be silly to be dogmatic on these complex matters, or to disagree with Hroch's contention that there is much more work to be done; none the less, I am inclined to argue that, even or especially in the light of evidence adduced by Hroch, it is the rival conclusion which does seem to be sustained by the facts.

This rival view could run something as follows: the pre-industrial world (feudalism/absolutism in Hroch's terminology) is endowed with a complex patchwork of cultures, and very diverse political formations. *Some* cultures pervade the ruling strata and the political apparatus of a state. These privileged cultures eventually define, in his terminology, 'great nations' (though actual size in the literal sense seems to be irrelevant). Other cultures (those of 'small' nations) are not so favourably located. They do not include rulers, and occupants of key political posts, among the practitioners of the said culture. So they must *create* their High Culture, before they could even strive for a state which would then protect it.

Hroch agrees that genuine modern nationalism does not occur in the earlier, pre-industrial stage, and that territorial movements ('Landespatriotismus') in this period should not be counted as a form of nationalism, contrary to the views of authors such as Hans Kohn (*Social Preconditions*, pp. 178 and 190). The real national principle comes to operate only in a new social order, with its greatly increased social mobility and the enormously increased importance of High, literate Culture. Hroch does not discuss interesting candidates for early, pre-modern nationalism, such as the Hussites.

The pre-industrial world is characterized by strata which, as it were, '*know* their place': in other words, *estates*. The industrial world by contrast is characterized by strata which do *not* know their place, in other words, by 'classes'. Their places are not frozen. If this transition is the essence of the 'bourgeois revolution', then such a revolution, at any rate, really does occur. But is there any example of the series of transformations of class relations, as postulated by Marxism, actually being *completed*? And why should we treat it as independent of nationalism and of *its* phases?

What has in fact happened is that national revolutions did occur in those cases in which class and cultural differences overlapped: classes without cultural differences attained nothing, and cultural ('ethnic') differences without class differences seldom achieved much. It was only their *conflation* which had a true revolutionary potential. In Hroch's own words:

Class struggle on its own led to no revolutions, and national struggle without conflict between strata in a mobile industrial society was similarly ineffective, . . . conflicts of interest between classes and groups whose members were divided at the same time by the fact that they belonged to different linguistic groups had indisputable significance for the intensification of the national movement. The polarity of material contradictions therefore ran parallel to differences of nationality, and as a result of this conflicts of interest were articulated not (or not only) at the social and political level appropriate to them but at the level of national categories and demands. (p. 185)

So, class conflict really took off if aided by ethnic/cultural differences. But equally (pp. 185 and 186):

where the national movement . . . was not capable of introducing into national agitation . . . the interests of specific classes and groups . . . it was not capable of attaining success.

So national movements were only effective if sustained by class rivalry. So, classes without ethnicity are blind, but ethnicities without class are powerless. Neither classes nor nations on their own produce structural changes. It is only their conflation which does so, in the condition brought about by industrialism.

Or again (p. 189):

the members of the new intelligentsia of the oppressed nationality in as far as they did not assimilate – were faced with an obstacle which impeded . . . their chance of rising into a higher social position. As soon as membership of a small nation began to be interpreted . . . as a group handicap, it began to function as a source of transformation of the social antagonism into a national one. It is the presence of cultural barriers to the mobility inherent in industrial society which leads to social transformation. Industrial society leads not to class war but to the emergence of homogeneous nation states.

So, in the end, we are faced with a picture which in effect treats neither classes nor nations as given. Loose classes replace clearly defined and enforced estates under conditions of mobility, engendered by a growth-oriented market society. Cultural differences shift from being markers of status, to defining large anonymous masses, capable of collective sentiment and action. Neither of these, however, are permanent features of human society. But when they do overlap, they are liable to become politically explosive. The uneven diffusion of industrialization produces socio-economic inequalities which, when they overlap with cultural differences, grant them with political appeal.

Industrialism engenders mobile, culturally homogeneous units. It leads to nationalist revolutions when class and cultural differences overlap. Hroch's formal strategy of mapping these onto each other, as if they were really independent, is unworkable. Classes and social categories not endorsed by law or ritual are by-products of the move towards modernity. If accompanied by cultural markers they lead to conflict. Both class conflict and the unacceptability of culturally expressed stratification, are the products of industrialization, which only tolerates so to speak unconfirmed classes, or evenly diffused cultural idiosyncrasies, but which faces nationalist trouble when interest and idiosyncrasy converge. Conflict of interest and cultural difference are politically effective if, and only if, they are *jointly* present. Hroch himself spells this out. Class conflict on its own fails to engender revolutions. As the overwhelming majority of cultural differences unsustained by economic ones also fail to find political expression. So there is no case for reifying nations either. Before the event, we can only observe countless cultural differentiations which are no more than differentiations, and we cannot tell just which will turn into 'nations'. Many are called but few are chosen. *After* the event, we know which nation *happened* to crystallize, but this does not justify saying that the nation in question 'was there' from the start, ready to be 'awakened'. They were neither more nor less present than differences which never turned into national markers. So, neither national nor class ideology should be taken at face value. Both antagonistic classes and antagonistic nations are explicable, though not in Marxist fashion. They are only effective in conjunction. That is the truth of the matter.

Hroch's work is valuable not only for the outstanding and unrivalled richness of its empirical material, and the ingenious manner in which it is used for the deployment of the comparative method; it is also valuable for its underlying theoretical purpose. Its aim seems to me misguided, but the determined effort to implement it is valuable, precisely because it enables us to see its weaknesses. What Hroch in effect tries to do is to confer scholarly respectability on two of the great myths of the nineteenth and twentieth centuries, namely Marxism and nationalism. He does this by retaining the Marxist theory of historic stages (or a rather truncated segment thereof), and to relate it to a schema of national awakening, quite specially applicable to what we have called Europe's third time zone. The nationalist myth is also endorsed by attributing some kind of genuine independent and pre-existent reality to the nations which *did* succeed in 'waking up'.

This vision is in the end indefensible. History is *neither* the conflict of classes *nor* of nations. In general, it is rich in countless kinds of conflict and cultural nuance, not reducible to those two alleged basic forms of opposition. Under the impact of a certain kind of socio-economic form, best described as 'industrialism', both classes (loose and unhallowed and unstable strata in a market society) *and* nations (anonymous, self-conscious, culturally defined human categories with political pretensions) emerge, and become politically significant, and often engender changes in boundaries, *when they converge*. Economic tension, signalled and underscored by cultural differences is politically potent, and it radically re-orders the map. Neither economic tension nor cultural difference on its own, achieves anything, or at any rate, not much. Each of them is a product rather than a prime mover. The socio-economic base is decisive. (It leads to cultural homogeneity and to a *loose* stratification.) That much is true in Marxism, even if its more specific propositions are false.

The genuine reality underlying the historic development seems to me to be a transition between two quite different patterns of relation between culture and power. Each of these patterns is deeply rooted in the economic bases of the social order, though not in the way specified by Marxism.[17] In the pre-industrial world, very complex patterns of culture and power were intertwined, but did not converge so as to form national–political boundaries. Under industrialism, both culture and power is standardized, and they underwrite each other and they converge. Political units acquire sharply defined boundaries, which at the same time become boundaries of cultures. Each culture needs its own political roof, and states legitimate themselves primarily as protectors of culture (and of course as guarantors of economic growth). This is the overall pattern and we have sketched out the manner in which its specific manifestations differently appear in various parts of Europe.

So neither classes nor nations exist as the permanent furniture of history. Agrarian society is endowed with complex stratification and great cultural diversity, but neither of these engenders major and decisive groupings. Under industrialism, economic polarization occurs for a time, and cultural standardization occurs for a *longer* time. When they converge, they decisively transform the map. All in all, this theory is better compatible with Hroch's own excellent data than is his own formal theory, which attempts to perpetuate both the 'class' and the 'nation' interpretation of history. But we have no further need of either of these two myths.

---

[17]   On the Marxist ontology of nations and classes, see Roman Szporluk, *Communism and Nationalism*, Oxford University Press, New York and Oxford, 1988, and also ch. 1.

Index